W9-DBG-613

UNDERSTANDING
URSULA K. LE GUIN

Understanding Contemporary American Literature

Matthew J. Bruccoli, *Editor*

UNDERSTANDING
Ursula K.
LE GUIN

Revised Edition

by ELIZABETH CUMMINS

UNIVERSITY OF SOUTH CAROLINA PRESS

Research for this book was supported by a grant from the Weldon
Springs Humanities Seminar program of the University of Missouri.

Published in Columbia, South Carolina, by the
University of South Carolina Press

Manufactured in the United States of America

Library of Congress Cataloging-in-Publication Data

Understanding Ursula K. Le Guin / by Elizabeth Cummins.
p. cm.—(Understanding contemporary American literature)
Includes bibliographical references.
ISBN 0-87249-869–7 (pbk)
1. Le Guin, Ursula K., 1929– —Criticism and interpretation.
2. Fantastic fiction, American—History and criticism. I. Title
II. Series.
PS3562.E42Z6 1990
813'.54—dc20   89-70435
                                                                CIP

CONTENTS

EDITOR'S PREFACE

Understanding Contemporary American Literature has been planned as a series of guides or companions for students as well as good nonacademic readers. The editor and publisher perceive a need for these volumes because much of the influential contemporary literature makes special demands. Uninitiated readers encounter difficulty in approaching works that depart from the traditional forms and techniques of prose and poetry. Literature relies on conventions, but the conventions keep evolving; new writers form their own conventions—which in time may become familiar. Put simply, *UCAL* provides instruction in how to read certain contemporary writers—identifying and explicating their material, themes, use of language, point of view, structures, symbolism, and responses to experience.

The word *understanding* in the series title was deliberately chosen. Many willing readers lack an adequate understanding of how contemporary literature works; that is, what the author is attempting to express and the means by which it is conveyed. Although the criticism and analysis in the series have been aimed at a level of general accessibility, these introductory volumes are meant to be applied in conjunction with the works they cover. Thus they do not provide a substitute for the works and authors they introduce, but rather prepare the reader for more profitable literary experiences.

M. J. B.

UNDERSTANDING
URSULA K. LE GUIN

CHAPTER ONE

Understanding Ursula K. Le Guin

Biographical Sketch

Central to understanding the fiction of Ursula K. Le Guin (born in Berkeley, California, on 21 October 1929) is the recognition of the importance of world-building and the nature of the different worlds she builds. This diversity of worlds Le Guin explores in her fiction was perhaps engendered by her own experiences as the child of Alfred and Theodora Kroeber. Not only did she live in homes of contrasting environments—Berkeley and a northern California ranch, East and West coasts, Europe and the United States—she also experienced her parents' interest in studying different cultures.

Alfred Kroeber (1876–1960), anthropologist, and Theodora Kroeber (1897–1979), psychologist and writer, created homes for their four children which resonated with ideas of cultural variety. Alfred Kroeber was one of the founders of modern anthropology, showing by example both close, scientific field study (as in *Handbook*

1

of the Indians of California, 1925) and the broad, theoretical search for the cultural patterns shared by human societies (as in *Configurations of Culture Growth*, 1944). Theodora Kroeber ensured the survival of Native American tales (as in *The Inland Whale*, 1959) and made comprehensible (in *Ishi in Two Worlds*, 1961) the history of the lone Yahi survivor who wandered into the twentieth century in 1911. In a 1977 interview Le Guin discussed the general influence of her parents:

I think most of the influence they have had is temperamental, inherited—like a willingness to get outside of your own culture and also a sensitivity to how culture affects personality, which is what my father was concerned with. My father felt very strongly that you can never actually get outside your own culture. All you can do is try. I think that feeling sometimes comes out in my writing. My father studied real cultures and I make them up—in a way, it's the same thing.[1]

From the time Le Guin was a year old, she always has had two West Coast homes. During the school year home was near the University of California campus in Berkeley. During the summer months home was in the Napa Valley, sixty miles north of San Francisco. This house was, Le Guin's mother has written, "a complete world."[2] To both homes came visitors—anthropologists as famous as Le Guin's father, graduate students, Na-

UNDERSTANDING URSULA K. LE GUIN

tive Americans—speaking German, English, or one of several Indian languages.

With her father's relatives in New York, Le Guin also had an East Coast home. Educated at Berkeley High School, she chose to go East for her university education—a BA from Radcliffe College (1951), an MA (1952) and advanced graduate work at Columbia University. Her major research was in the world of French and Italian Renaissance poetry. Fulbright Scholarships allowed her to live in Paris (1953–54) and in London (1968–69 and 1975–76). Her marriage to Charles Le Guin in December 1953 led eventually to the establishment of her own home in Portland, Oregon, where the Le Guins have raised their three children, often taking them to the family land in the Napa Valley for summer vacations.

The common activity at all of these homes for Le Guin was writing. She has said that she did not decide to become a writer because she has always been a writer.[3] Her publishing career began in 1958 with a book review, then several poems in little magazines, a short story in 1961, and the first commercial story in 1962. An examination of her list of publications reveals that the most intense period of writing and publication has been 1966–1974, during which she published seven science fiction novels, three fantasy novels, sixteen short stories, nine poems, five book reviews, and sixteen essays.

UNDERSTANDING URSULA K. LE GUIN

Recognition came early in this intense period. In 1969 her first fantasy novel, *A Wizard of Earthsea,* won the Boston Globe-Horn Book Award, and in 1970 she won both the Hugo and Nebula Awards for her fourth science fiction novel, *The Left Hand of Darkness.* Additional awards followed, including more Hugos and Nebulas, and the National Book Award in 1973 for *The Farthest Shore.*

The fiction of 1966–1974 is that for which she is best known, the great journeys of time and space either through the islands that make up the Earthsea world of her fantasy novels or the many planets of the Hainish world of her science fiction. After 1974 Le Guin has used the great journeys far less frequently. Her short stories, novels, and poems are rooted in Orsinia, an imaginary central European country she created as a young adult, or in the lands of the West Coast, either in the present or future time.

Both Le Guin's biography and her publications reveal that she has always been at home in more than one world.

Overview

Ursula K. Le Guin suggests the importance of "world" in the following description of how she begins a novel: "A person [is] seen, seen at a certain distance, usually in a landscape. The place is there, the person is there. I didn't invent him, I didn't make her up: he or she is there. And my business is to get there too."[4]

Writing a novel for Le Guin, then, begins with an image of place and person. Place and person are somehow related; if Le Guin sees one, she also sees the other. The act of seeing them establishes a relationship between herself and the world so that she feels it is her "business" to get "there," to decrease the distance between person and place by getting to know and understand them. The perception of self and other, the ability to distinguish between "me" and "not-me," is a recognition of both difference and affinity.

The journey from here to there, from self to other, is also taken by the reader. Le Guin is the guide with whom the readers interact as they try to see what she calls to their attention. They become used to her signals: they explore not only her fictional world but their own world as well. They are changed by the journey; they "see" here and there, or homeland and foreign land, differently. They "see" self and other, native and alien, differently for the same reason. The readers question the nature of home, the nature of alien, "who we are, and where we are, and what choices face us."[5] Casual readers and demanding critics alike have praised Le Guin for her ability to make worlds in words. Her style, often called lyrical, results from her sensitivity to sound and syntax, from her wit and wisdom as she plays with and invents language.

UNDERSTANDING URSULA K. LE GUIN

During her apprenticeship years Le Guin realized that the genres best suited for depicting this journey of discovery undertaken by both author and reader were science fiction and fantasy. On a commercial level they were, and still are, categories which publishers recognize and can market; therefore Le Guin was able to sell her manuscripts readily.[6] But more importantly, they are genres in which world-building is essential. Although readers and critics differ widely on the definitions of these two genres, the definitions of science fiction writer and critic Samuel Delany are useful. Delany says that if a report describes what happened and a realistic novel describes what "could have happened," then science fiction describes what has not happened and fantasy describes what "could not have happened."[7] Le Guin's metaphor of the spectrum is also helpful for distinguishing between science fiction and fantasy literature.[8] At one end of this linear spectrum is the purest science fiction; at the other end, the purest fantasy; along the line any number of varieties is possible, but eventually one form shades into the other. Science fiction and fantasy share the same spectrum because they both create worlds that are radically different from the author's "consensus reality," that is, the facts and beliefs about the world of the author and of the reader on which people base their daily activities.[9] The created or alternate world violates consensus reality in such things as intelligent life forms, language, history, atmospheric conditions, or physical location.

UNDERSTANDING URSULA K. LE GUIN

The worlds of science fiction and fantasy literature, then, offer readers a chance to stretch their minds by experiencing an alternate world and then a chance to return to consensus reality with a changed perspective. For example, the reader may see that technological progress can destroy the environment, that mathematics is a tool that constructs more than it describes reality, or that the way one individual deals with an alien other is finally what determines the nature of the society.

Science fiction and fantasy belong at opposite ends of the spectrum because they differ in how they derive their alternate worlds from consensus reality. Science fiction's alternate world is derived by supposing a radical difference from some organized body of scientific knowledge, including both the "hard" sciences (such as physics, chemistry, or geology) and the "soft" sciences (such as anthropology, psychology, or history). The radical difference may be the existence of a colossal sentient computer, a time machine, a culture without war, or a human race in which each individual can function sexually as either male or female. Once this difference is posited, however, the work rigorously uses science—both the body of knowledge and the method of inquiry—to make the world seem possible.

Fantasy's alternate world is derived by supposing a radical difference from the rational foundation of all knowledge, by supposing the existence of supernatural forces which suffuse the daily activities of the world. The radical difference may be incredible characters such as hobbits, talking animals, ancient and wise dragons, or magic-workers such as sorcerers and wizards. Compared to the world of consensus reality, science fiction creates an alternate world that might be possible, whereas fantasy creates an alternate world that is impossible.

It might be helpful to try to place on this spectrum the four worlds that Le Guin has used for nearly all of her published fiction to date—Earthsea, the Hainish planets, Orsinia, and the American West Coast in the near future. Near the fantasy end would be Earthsea. This world is an archipelago, a group of islands raised from the sea when the ancient deity/epic hero Segoy spoke the word of creation. Inhabited by dragons, ordinary people, and wizards and sorcerers, it is a world where magic works. At the opposite end of the spectrum would be the Hainish planets. Although widely different, all of the nearly one hundred Hainish planets can support human life and were "seeded" with life, possibly a million years ago, by the ancient people of the planet Hain. The difference among the words, their inhabitants, and their technologies are explained by scientific or pseudoscientific concepts. Orsinia is a landlocked country in Central Europe. It might be placed midway between the science fiction end and the spectrum's center, for although the alternate world is scientifically accounted for, it "fantastically" coexists in space *and* time with consensus reality. The American West Coast—northern California, Oregon, and Washing-

UNDERSTANDING URSULA K. LE GUIN

ton—is the locale for Le Guin's speculative stories about America's future. The western edge of these contiguous states, suggesting the possibility of an end or a beginning, is an appropriate setting for her apocalyptic visions. It might be placed nearly at the spectrum's center, for although it is clearly a science fiction world, it includes a spiritual realm that is almost as tangible as the magic in Earthsea.

Earthsea, the world of Le Guin's trilogy of fantasy novels, is an appropriate place to begin an overview of her worlds, for it makes concrete her essential principles of world-building and of the relationship between the human and physical worlds. The Earthsea books (*A Wizard of Earthsea*, 1968; *The Tombs of Atuan*, 1971; and *The Farthest Shore*, 1972) are a trilogy, three novels linked chronologically as they follow a common character, Ged, from adolescence to old age, and linked thematically as they explore the experience of coming of age— for Ged in the first novel, an adolescent priestess in the second, and an Earthsea prince in the third.

As fantasy Earthsea is a world of dragons and wizards, a world in which magic works for both good and evil. As its name suggests, it is a "both/and" world, one formed out of both land and sea, depending on the balancing between both earth and sea, between its people and their environment. Its people acknowledge the delicate balance that exists among all things; they call it the Equilibrium, and know that the wizards and mages can change that balance. In each of the three novels

UNDERSTANDING URSULA K. LE GUIN

Le Guin's common character, Ged, encounters situations where his magic spells (his use of language) can maintain, disturb, or right the balance.

This world of land and sea, outside of consensus reality, is Le Guin's concrete image for the idea that all things—organic and inorganic, material and spiritual, object and force—shape and are shaped by each other.

The coming-of-age experiences depicted in each of the Earthsea novels represent journeys that are both physical and psychological. The crucial encounter for each of the three protagonists is with the temptations of the powers of darkness. The adolescents in each of the three novels are aided by wise men who teach them that part of becoming an adult is learning that they are an integral part of the network of existence which they must learn to respect by coming to know not merely the use of each thing but also its essence, its uniqueness.

The reader who completes Le Guin's fantasy trilogy returns from the journey through the text with a heightened awareness of the nature of the coming-of-age experience, of the interdependency of person and place, and of the significance of language. If the coming-of-age experience is thought of as a hero's quest, then the reader wrestles with a new aspect of the hero, the ability to know when not to act. Further, the reader has a new model to consider for the quest. It is not a single, adventurous journey but rather a lifelong journey from adolescence to old age through a series of changes. In

UNDERSTANDING URSULA K. LE GUIN

addition to questioning the coming-of-age experience, the reader also reexamines the human relationship with the environment and the human ability to know and affect that reality. Le Guin's Earthsea emphasizes the interdependency among all existing things, certainly an ongoing concern for this planet and its advanced technological societies which make holes in the ozone layer, create radioactive fallout, oil slicks, and endangered species. Her world also emphasizes language, the human tool for learning about and affecting the environment as well as each other. The wizard's power of naming, the reader realizes, symbolizes the power of language to make reality; it is a tool by which humans participate in, cooperate with, or control reality.

In contrast to the fantasy world of Earthsea where magic works and the tenuous balance of all·existence is crucial, Le Guin's science fiction world underscores the importance of maintaining a balance among the peoples of the Hainish planets by recognizing the commonality of humanity within the different races and cultures. The radical differences within the Hainish world are indicated by the fact that there are eighty-four different planets that have been settled or "seeded" by the ancient Hains or by their ancestors. Consequently, though all the planets are different environments and different cultures, their inhabitants all share a common ancestor, the Hains. To date Le Guin has published six Hainish novels: *Rocannon's World* (1966), *Planet of Exile* (1966),

UNDERSTANDING URSULA K. LE GUIN

City of Illusions (1967), *The Left Hand of Darkness* (1969), *The Word for World is Forest* (1972), and *The Dispossessed* (1974). The last three works are considered her major science fiction novels.

Although the Hainish planets are, like Earthsea, outside of consensus reality, the environmental characteristics of the planets and their human communities are validated by the sciences of biology, psychology, physics, and, most importantly, by anthropology. In these novels Le Guin's protagonists are usually ethnologists or anthropologists who study the natures of different cultures. Because of the immensity and diversity of the Hainish world, communication and understanding become vital. Consequently Le Guin's futuristic scientists have developed tools for enhancing communication such as faster-than-light spaceships and a device called the ansible, which makes communication across distances of light years instantaneous. Additionally, nearly all the inhabitants have the ability to communicate through what Le Guin calls mindhearing and mindspeech, a sort of instantaneous mindreading.

The Hainish novels focus on the significance of diplomacy, the struggle to balance conflicting needs of the human community and of the individual. They deal with the opposition between freedom and social restriction, between loyalty and betrayal, and between alienation and integration. The immense and diverse physical environment Le Guin establishes necessitates the plot

UNDERSTANDING URSULA K. LE GUIN

device shared with the Earthsea novels: the voyage of discovery that leads to knowledge of the other and to knowledge of the self.

Her protagonists come to a new world as representatives of their home planet. Encountering strange cultures, they find themselves being called "alien," or even "pervert." The protagonists must reexamine their own sense of humanness, world, and home and are forced to recognize that these "aliens" are also human. The antagonists in the Hainish stories are almost always men who seek personal power and gratification regardless of the effects on the freedom of others or on the nature of the community. Because the protagonists are also diplomats, their struggle assumes epic proportions. If the individual aliens can establish a community of two, then there is hope for relationships between the two planets.

Although the protagonist is transformed by experience, Le Guin always concludes her novel without depicting what relationships will develop between the two worlds. So the reader comes away from one or several novels of the Hainish world with a heightened awareness of the experience of alienation, the complexities of trying to communicate with the stranger, and the shock as well as delight of an encounter with an alternative way of looking at the world.

After the spatial expansiveness of Le Guin's science fiction, Orsinia seems like a very small, cramped world.

UNDERSTANDING URSULA K. LE GUIN

Orsinia is embedded—both geographically and historically—in Central Europe. Even though it was invented before Le Guin's other worlds, it is less familiar to readers than are Earthsea and the Hainish planets. Le Guin's first published short story was about Orsinia (1961), but this world was not recognized until she published *Orsinian Tales* (1976), an anthology of short stories, and *Malafrena* (1979), a novel. Unlike the worlds of Earthsea and the Hainish novels Orsinia is a world without obvious science fiction or fantasy features. Yet, like the Hainish planets and Earthsea, Orsinia does not exist in consensus reality.

Orsinia is, in Le Guin's own words, "an invented though nonfantastic Central European country."[10] It is small and landlocked, like modern-day Hungary and Czechoslovakia. It has its own language, and for centuries has been divided into ten provinces. It shares with other European countries a feudal period, a struggle for unity under a single king, periods of being conquered and ruled by foreign governments, the impetus of the French revolutions to struggle away from a monarchy and into a republic, and participation in World Wars I and II. So, unlike the Hainish world where each new planet is given the opportunity to join a larger human community, Orsinians have been the victims of imperialistic aggression by larger human communities. Again and again they have lost their independence, and yet they have maintained a fierce love for their ethnic identity and their land.

15

UNDERSTANDING URSULA K. LE GUIN

The word *Orsinia* and Le Guin's first name, Ursula, share the same word root, and she has said that Orsinia is her country.[11] As if expressing her own European heritage, which was closely tied to German and Polish culture and to specific locations (her Kroeber ancestors came from the village of Kroebern in Germany and her Kracaw ancestors came from Cracow),[12] Le Guin creates characters who choose to remain in their homeland, even though they are politically, economically, socially oppressed. On an even larger scale the Orsinian stories also express the Central European heritage in the Western world. Orsinia is in the middle of some of the most tumultuous events in Western civilization—the French Revolution, the general shift from absolute governments to republics, Hitler's rise to power, the Holocaust, World War II, the threat of nuclear war.

Unlike her science fiction and fantasy, here journeys are only contemplated or are confined within Orsinia's borders—a day's train ride, a walk across the city, or at most a trip from the mountains to the capital city. The plots, too, are "confined"; the stories explore how individuals reconcile their desire for freedom or development (psychological, artistic, economic, political) with the facts of their oppression. The stories climax and end with a moment of insight or recognition for the main characters; but what the characters' lives will be like after this moment of insight is unknown. Her protagonists are unlike those of the science fiction and fantasy stories who, in spite of their personal humility and unpretentiousness, appear at the right place and at the right time. The science fiction and fantasy protagonists are heroic because they bring a perspective that changes the nature of the alien culture and world with which they interact. The Orsinian protagonists are farmers, landowners, publishers, soldiers, quarry laborers, artists, scientists, who are not legends-in-the-making, whose single act will not immediately change the course of history or stop the next wave of imperialistic aggression or the next war. In their daily lives, however, they demonstrate how to survive and yet maintain dignity.

The Orsinian tales affect the reader's perspective on history. Though they suggest some of the most horrendous events in Western culture, the tales remind the reader that history is not only great events and rulers' decisions; it is also decisions of the individual to attain freedom to think, to write, to define oneself, to choose one's home or lifework or partner.

Like the world of Orsinia, the scale of the future West Coast is also limited. Although Le Guin had published *The Lathe of Heaven* (1971) and "The New Atlantis" (1975), it was not until the publication of *Always Coming Home* in 1985 that it became clear a fourth world, the future American West Coast, existed in Le Guin's fiction.

Despite their shared setting these three works do not function as a trilogy; there are no common characters and little shared history, although each assumes a

UNDERSTANDING URSULA K. LE GUIN

past industrial, urban, capitalistic society like that of the contemporary United States. However, all three are science fiction. Le Guin sets all three stories in the twenty-first century and makes the nature of the coast and human society credible through the sciences of meteorology, geology, anthropology, and dream study. The future coast has been reshaped by natural disasters (earthquake, volcanic eruption, flooding), and its resources have been damaged by human disasters (war, radiation leakage, industrial waste).

The main characters in these works experience the most drastic alienation of any of Le Guin's science fiction characters. Rather than making the long space journey to a world which they expect to be alien, these characters have no way to leave earth and must experience their own homeland becoming a strange land. For an author whose novels begin with the image of person and place, homeworld catastrophes would seem to be the most difficult settings and plots Le Guin could undertake. In a 1982 interview she stated that *The Lathe of Heaven* and "The New Atlantis" "are among the saddest things I've written, the nearest to not being hopeful, and they're both set right here [Portland]."[13] In *The Lathe of Heaven*, George Orr is at the center of the changes, for it is his effective dreams which initially halt total destruction of the world in nuclear war and then continue to change the nature of society. In "The New Atlantis," Belle tries to cope with the knowledge of disaster coming—her homeland will be inundated. *Always Coming Home* is a postdisaster novel and features a culture which has learned to reconnect with its changed homeland.

These works reflect Le Guin's concern with the shape her contemporary world seems to be taking; behind them are the extermination of California Indian tribes, the Jewish displacement and holocaust, the incarceration of the Japanese Americans in California during World War II, and Hiroshima with all its portents for a nonfuture. Although Le Guin has continually carried on a quarrel with the concept of the planned utopia in her fiction, the fourth world is the only one where she overtly considers the issues of utopia in all of the works set there. *The Lathe of Heaven* and "The New Atlantis" portray the failure of a planned utopia to provide greater material comfort, freedom, or happiness for its citizens. *Always Coming Home* rejects the traditional utopia as a place where all people are permanently happy (at the expense of freedom) and where life is easy. Instead it offers a society where people work hard, struggle against disease and a high infant mortality rate, fear being conquered by their warlike neighbors, but also where people practice conservation, moderation, and government by consent.

The reader experiences dislocation and alienation as each of these works presents a skewed map of the familiar western coastline. Not only have the lines of the coast been redrawn, but the lines that might represent

UNDERSTANDING URSULA K. LE GUIN

the future shape of American society have also been redrawn. Each of the three works, suggests a different twenty-first century America, culminating in *Always Coming Home* with a society whose decisions are not based on the necessity of growth and the belief in progress.

A way of changing a society's beliefs in ideas such as these is made explicit in *Always Coming Home;* that way is storytelling. There has been no culture, Le Guin has stated, that did not tell stories. A world's stories embody not only its current tensions, stresses, conflicts, and values but also its ability to dream of alternative ways of doing things, alternative political structures, environmental policies, and values. In *Always Coming Home*, a novel which speaks with many narrative voices, Le Guin suggests that if American culture is embodied in its stories, then one way to change its headlong dash toward nuclear war and depletion of natural resources is to change the stories. If people can imagine an alternate world here on this planet, and imagine its inhabitants, then they have increased their chances of getting there.

As this overview of Le Guin's fictional worlds suggests, "getting there" is a journey for both artist and reader. The journey may occur within the expansive worlds of Earthsea or the Hainish planets or within the restricted worlds of Orsinia or the American West Coast. An individual journey may become an exploration of the coming-of-age process that lasts a lifetime, or of alienation and connection, or of the difficulties of identifying one's inheritance, or of the nature of utopia. Whatever world, whatever journey, the reader will be immersed in a new "there," which will lead to a better understanding of intelligent beings, the world, and the interaction between the two.

Notes

1. Win McCormack and Anne Mendel, "Creating Realistic Utopias," *Seven Days* 11 Apr. 1977: 39.

2. Theodora Kroeber, *Alfred Kroeber: A Personal Configuration* (Berkeley: University of California, 1971) 141.

3. Le Guin, "A Citizen of Mondath," *The Language of the Night*, ed. Susan Wood (New York: Putnam's, 1979) 26–28.

4. Le Guin, "Science Fiction and Mrs. Brown," *Language of the Night* 110.

5. "Science Fiction and Mrs. Brown" 118.

6. "A Citizen of Mondath" 28.

7. Samuel R. Delany, "About Five Thousand One Hundred and Seventy Five Words," *SF: The Other Side of Realism*, ed. Thomas D. Clareson (Bowling Green, OH: Bowling Green University Popular Press, 1971) 141.

8. Le Guin, "Introduction to *Rocannon's World*," *Language of the Night* 133. Eric S. Rabkin also uses the spectrum to help define fantasy and science fiction; see his *The Fantastic in Literature* (Princeton: Princeton University Press, 1976).

9. Kathryn Hume, *Fantasy and Mimesis: Responses to Reality in Western Literature* (New York: Methuen, 1984) xi. For an overview of the definitions of science fiction see Brian Stableford and Peter

UNDERSTANDING URSULA K. LE GUIN

Nicholls, "Definitions of SF," *The Science Fiction Encyclopedia* (Garden City, NY: Doubleday, 1979) 159–61. Essential for understanding the relationship between modern science and narrative structure is Frank Sadler, *The Unified Ring: Narrative Art and the Science-Fiction Novel* (Ann Arbor, MI: UMI Research Press, 1984).

    10. "A Citizen of Mondath" 28.

    11. James W. Bittner, *Approaches to the Fiction of Ursula K. Le Guin* (Ann Arbor, MI: UMI Research Press, 1984) 29.

    12. Kroeber, 5, 121.

    13. Larry McCaffery and Sinda Gregory, "An Interview with Ursula Le Guin," *The Missouri Review* 7, no. 2 (1984): 76.

CHAPTER TWO

Earthsea

The impetus for the Earthsea series was Le Guin's invitation in 1967 from Herbert Schein, publisher of Parnassus Press, to write a book for an adolescent audience. That audience, Le Guin explains in her essay "Dreams Must Explain Themselves" (1973), led to her choosing the main theme of coming of age and the genre of fantasy. "Coming of age," she writes, "is a process that took me many years; I finished it, so far as I ever will, at about age thirty-one; and so I feel rather deeply about it. So do most adolescents. It's their main occupation, in fact."[1] In the trilogy Le Guin narrates the coming-of-age process as a journey into the self. In the same essay she says, "Fantasy is the medium best suited to a description of that journey, its perils and rewards. The events of a voyage into the unconscious are not describable in the language of rational daily life: only the symbolic language of the deeper psyche will fit them without trivializing them."[2] (Le Guin's comments and the discussion in this chapter refer to the trilogy; the fourth novel, *Tehanu: The Last Book of Earthsea*, is scheduled for release in 1990.)

EARTHSEA

Fantasy, in other words, like myth and dream, assumes the existence of a world of being beyond or underneath perceived, empirical reality; and it reproduces that other world by means of symbol and literary archetype. Wizards, shadows, dragons, a labyrinth, ring, dragon, and sword are some of the symbols and archetypes that reverberate with ethical, emotional, and aesthetic meaning in Le Guin's fantasy trilogy.

These archetypes and symbols can carry such meaning because, as she relates in her essay "The Child and the Shadow" (1975), "we all have the same general tendencies and configurations in our psyche."[3] The idea of shared psychic roots is based on Carl Gustav Jung's psychology. Jung argued that beyond the conscious mind there lay two other mental activities—the individual unconscious, which is unique to each person, and the collective unconscious, which is shared by all people. The symbols and archetypes that are common to myths throughout the world are the manifestations of the collective unconscious. The myths were stories that connected the unconscious and the conscious, stories that used symbols and images to connect the desires and fears and hopes and creativity of the unconscious to the conscious mind.

Such a connection is made during that journey into the unconscious which is part of the adolescent's coming of age. Le Guin believes that a primary characteristic of such a journey is that it is "not only a psychic one, but a moral one," one that "contain[s] a very strong, striking moral dialectic"[4] between the potential for good and for evil within the self. The goal of this psychic and moral journey is, in Le Guin's words, the hope that the journeyer "will be less inclined, perhaps, either to give up in despair or to deny what he sees, when he must face the evil that is done in the world, and the injustices and grief and suffering that we all must bear."[5]

This kind of fantasy exemplifies what Francis J. Molson calls "ethical fantasy." It is a fiction that both delights and instructs its audience. Specifically, Molson asserts, it

dramatizes several interrelated propositions whose continuing validity is taken for granted: making ethical choices, whether deliberate or not, is central in the lives of young people; actions do bear consequences not only for oneself but for society . . . ; maturity involves accepting responsibility for one's actions; and character bespeaks destiny. Ethical fantasy, moreover, is a symbolization of these propositions which does not usually endorse or reflect explicitly any particular religion, sect, or ideology.[6]

A Wizard of Earthsea was written as a single novel; apart from J. R. R. Tolkien's *Lord of the Rings,* trilogies were not common in fantasy and science fiction. The loose ends of the first novel, Le Guin records, led her to write *The Tombs of Atuan.* Another year, more thought, and she published a third novel, *The Farthest*

EARTHSEA

Shore.[7] The coming-of-age story was so central to her use of fantasy that each of the other two novels also features a young protagonist who crosses the threshold into adulthood. But as her imagination kept returning to Earthsea, two additional subjects emerged. One was the complete life story of Ged, the only character who appears in all three novels. Embedded in his story was the other subject, artistry, "the creative experience, the creative process."[8]

Le Guin first used Earthsea as a fictional setting in two short stories published in 1964, "The Word of Unbinding" and "The Rule of Names," and in an unpublished story written in 1965 or 1966.[9] Earthsea is an archipelago populated by people, wizards, and dragons; it is a place where magic works. Although Earthsea is a kingdom, its islands are separated and different enough in resources and climate that each has a sense of independence and an awareness that some independence must be sacrificed to make a unified kingdom. Beyond this dynamic relationship between individual island and aggregate kingdom is the dynamism of natural forces suggested in the archipelago's name, Earthsea. The balance of the powers of the physical landscape is a manifestation of still another level of balanced forces, a cosmic balance which the people of Earthsea call the Equilibrium. They speak of the world as being "in balance"; the act of creation is described as a "balancing of the dark and the light"; and they look to the Archmage, the highest ranking wizard to "watch the Equilibrium."[10]

A world, then, is not just the tangible elements of place, nature, humankind, culture; it is also a process, a creative relationship among all things that exist—physical and spiritual, natural and human. Le Guin's concept of a world exhibits ideas compatible with those of both twentieth-century anthropologists and twentieth-century physicists. Much of her father's early field work among Native Americans in California revealed stories that stress an intimate relationship between nature and human society. This relationship has also been expressed by Werner Heisenberg, who asserted that in modern physics "there appears above all the network of relationships between men and nature, of the connections through which we as physical beings are dependent parts of nature and at the same time, as human beings, make them the object of our thought and actions."[11] This "network of relationships" is a metaphor Le Guin suggests in her choice of earth and sea as the world of her fantasy trilogy.

The principle of balanced powers, the recognition that every act affects self, society, world, and cosmos, is both a physical and a moral principle of Le Guin's fantasy world. The people of Earthsea honor the Equilibrium in their dances, songs, and rituals performed at the winter and summer solstices when the sun appears to change direction. They believe that their participation assists the movements of the cosmos and ensures the

sun's return. The people with magic powers, from archmage to village witch, can directly influence the Equilibrium if they know the "true" name of that which they
wish to change. Naming is the key to magic; to know
the true name of anything is to know its essence and
thus be able to control it. Humans honor the acquisition
of names. When each girl or boy reaches puberty, part
of the passage ceremony is being given a true name,
which is told only to the most trusted friends. The creative power of naming in wizardry is analogous to the
creative power of word use in the art of fiction.

A wizard like Earthsea's protagonist Ged spends
his life learning the words and spells, which can affect
the balance, and learning the consequences of acting.
As Ged explains to the young prince Arren:

Do you see, Arren, how an act is not, as young men
think, like a rock that one picks up and throws, and it
hits or misses, and that's the end of it. When that rock
is lifted, the earth is lighter; the hand that bears it heav-
ier. When it is thrown, the circuits of the stars respond,
and where it strikes or falls the universe is changed.
On every act the balance of the whole depends.[12]

During the thirty or forty years covered by the trilogy Earthsea is a world which is out of balance. The
kingdom has not had a king for some eight hundred
years; disrespect for the mages, for the principle of balanced powers, and for the kingdom itself has grown on

certain islands. The new king, it has been prophesied, will be he *"who has crossed the dark land living and come to the far shores of the day."*[13]

The world Le Guin discovered in her imagination is appropriate for the three subjects she wished to explore. This is not to suggest that she methodically worked out the details of the world to fit the themes she wanted to discuss. Given her insistence that in order to create fiction the writer also journeys into the unconscious, one can say only that the world, characters, and themes are all interwoven. The concept of the Equilibrium dramatizes the significance of the individual's coming of age, for knowledge of the self and of the potential to do good or evil is essential for protecting the delicate balance of cosmos, kingdom, and community—hence three coming-of-age stories. To restore balance to the kingdom requires a lengthy tale of a great hero—hence Ged's story from youth to old age. The power by which magicians can affect the world is activated by words—hence the magician doubles as the creative and transforming artist.

Coming-of-Age Stories

Readers have documented the parallels between Earthsea's coming-of-age process and myths, fairy tales, and Jungian psychology. Margaret P. Esmonde, for example, argued that the "master pattern" for the trilogy is the psychological journey to selfhood as discussed by Jung. The adolescent has a frightening confrontation with the dark side of the self (imaged as the shadow), followed by experiences which culminate in a recognition scene that signals the achievement of an integrated personality.[14] Richard F. Patteson delineates the parallels between the plot structure of the trilogy and fairy tales (testing of the hero, conflict, and victory) and argues, following Bruno Bettelheim, that "fairy tales help children work out feelings of helplessness and insecurity; they aid them in discovering their identity and developing their character; they teach them that life's inevitable conflicts can be overcome."[15] In her essays Le Guin explained the similarities among myths and fairy tales on the basis of their common source, the collective unconscious. Many of the best-known students of myth and archetype have relied on the same body of myths and tales; therefore a critic must be careful to offer substantial evidence when privileging one over the others in interpreting Le Guin's work. All are helpful to some degree: Carl Jung, Bruno Bettelheim, Joseph Campbell, Northrop Frye, Mircea Eliade, Sir James Frazer.

Although Le Guin used Jung to help explain the power of fantasy, she has asserted on several occasions that she had not read Jung until after she had published the Earthsea trilogy.[16] Readers who are interested in the stories Le Guin read should look at fairy tales by Hans Christian Andersen and the Brothers Grimm and myths told in Lady Frazer's *Leaves from the Golden Bough*, Padraic Colum's *The Children of Odin*, and Sir James Frazer's *The Golden Bough*.[17]

Each of the three novels presents the process of coming of age for a different character, in a different context, and with different results. In *A Wizard of Earthsea* Ged must learn to discipline his innate power of magic and understand the need for discipline. His psychological journey is mirrored in his physical journey from the heart of Earthsea out to its western and eastern edges. In *The Tombs of Atuan* the young priestess Tenar must break free of the role imposed on her by her society and join the larger human community of Earthsea. Her trapped self is mirrored in the walled-in religious center where she lives. In *The Farthest Shore* the young prince Arren must achieve the courage, self-reliance, and self-knowledge to become the first king of Earthsea in eight hundred years. Arren's psychological journey is also a physical journey; he sails from the heart of Earthsea west into the uncharted sea and then enters the land of the dead.

A Wizard of Earthsea is, of the three novels, the most complete account of coming of age as a journey into the self; its protagonist is one of the kingdom's greatest wizards. So private is this journey it is not included in the public celebration of his life, the *Deed of Ged*. In his journey from adolescence to adulthood Ged acquires psychological and moral knowledge about his innate power of wizardry. The journey is intensified when,

EARTHSEA

motivated by pride, he uses his powers to call up a spirit from the dead; the resulting crisis affects Ged and the safety of those who associate with him. For the straight-forward narrative of Ged's life, from about age seven to nineteen, Le Guin uses an omniscient point of view. This allows her to use the opening and closing paragraphs of the novel to establish a context for Ged's maturation. The reader learns not only that Ged's quest is successful, but that he eventually achieves the highest mage's rank, Archmage of Earthsea. *A Wizard of Earthsea* is in the tradition of the apprenticeship novel *(Bildungsroman)*, which traces the development of a young person's awareness of self, society, and nature. Particularly the novel is a male *Bildungsroman*, for Ged achieves a socially sanctioned and acclaimed role.

Like the early life of the mythic hero Ged's child-hood includes revelations of his extraordinary power. Ged learns that he has the potential to control both him-self and the external world. All he needs to learn, he believes, is the how—the words, runes, spells, and ges-tures. After successfully weaving a fog which hides and protects his village from the warriors of Kargad, how-ever, Ged is unable to resume his daily life. Ogion re-stores Ged and names him: he identifies him as a "mageborn," and at the ceremony of passage he gives Ged his true name.

As he begins his apprenticeship with Ogion, Ged exhibits the universal desire of the adolescent to control self and environment for self-gratification:

UNDERSTANDING URSULA K. LE GUIN

Ged had thought that as the prentice of a great mage he would enter at once into the mystery and mastery of power. He would understand the language of the beasts and the speech of the leaves of the forest, he thought, and sway the winds with his word, and learn to change himself into any shape he wished. Maybe he and his master would run together as stags, or fly to Re Albi over the mountain on the wings of eagles.[18]

Self-transformation means an external shape change; and Ged imagines that if he could change his shape, he would thereby be part of a world in which he is freer or more powerful or more admired. As his actions under Ogion's tutelage bear out, Ged has not recognized that the most significant self-development will come from knowing his internal self—his desires, his capability for evil and for good, his pride.

At the School for Wizards on Roke, Ged learns of the nature and ethics of power. He is warned by Master Hand:

But you must not change one thing, one pebble, one grain of sand, until you know what good and evil will follow on that act. The world is in balance, in Equilibrium. A wizard's power of Changing and of Summoning can shake the balance of the world. It is dangerous, that power. It is most perilous. It must follow knowledge, and serve need. To light a candle is to cast a shadow (44).

Such warnings do not speak as loudly to Ged as his own
inner voice of pride does; he thinks, "But surely a wizard . . . was powerful enough to do what he pleased,
and balance the world as seemed best to him, and drive
back darkness with his own light" (44).

"To light a candle is to cast a shadow" is a metaphor
for the idea that opposites are actually complementary.
To explain fantasy's frequent use of light and darkness
as symbols of good and evil, Le Guin uses the yang-yin
symbol, an ancient Chinese pictograph of the integration of opposites :

Evil, then, appears in the fairy tale not as something
diametrically opposed to good, but as inextricably involved with it, as in the yang-yin symbol. Neither is
greater than the other, nor can human reason and virtue
separate one from the other and choose between them.
The hero or heroine is the one who sees what is appropriate to be done, because he or she sees the *whole*,
which is greater than either evil or good. Their heroism
is, in fact, their certainty. They do not act by rules; they
simply know the way to go.[19]

The yang-yin symbol is common to Taoism (the
only religion Le Guin has admitted to) and other ancient
Chinese philosophies. Yin and yang are the primal
forces out of whose interaction arises the world of being. The symbol expresses the operations of Tao, the
inexhaustible, self-creating principle of the universe. As

the two halves appear to be in unstable balance, the symbol expresses the Taoist belief that all existence is in a state of change, flux, and transformation. But the symbol also suggests unity because both are held within the circle's boundary and in each is contained the germ of the other. All existence, from the cosmic to the personal, is seen as consisting of complementary opposites, such as being and becoming, duration and creation, essence and change, male and female.

In Western thought light and dark are often regarded as symbols of the dualistic, warring powers of good and evil. Such dualism suggests that the world consists of hierarchical relationships and that self and other (defined as that which is different; e.g., in culture, race, sex, religion) is always a relationship of competition and power.

Ged misuses his power in the duel with Jasper because he is more interested in demonstrating his personal power than he is in respecting the interrelationship of light and darkness. Not fully understanding what he sought nor the effect of his powers, Ged allowed his conscious mind to call up Elfarren while his unconscious mind simultaneously attracted the shadow. The shadow, a common image in fairy tales, is a literary archetype for that integral part of the self which the immature individual tries to deny. So important is one's confrontation with the shadow to the process of growing up that Jung, Le Guin notes in "The Child and the Shadow," identified it as the guide for the journey into the self. The shadow is "all the qualities and tendencies within us which have been repressed, denied, or not used."[20] The shadow symbolizes Ged's unrecognized pride, desire for power and control, and fear of his own death.

Although the shadow is Ged's personal adversary, its emergence and disappearance have far-reaching consequences. The remaining two-thirds of the novel tells the story of Ged's quest to avoid the shadow and then to find and name it. The episodes test his wizardry and initiate him into his socially approved role as one of Earthsea's greatest mages. Specifically, Ged's initiation includes knowledge of the trust and betrayal in human society; of evil and death; of the wisdom and power of nature; and of his own arrogance, denial, fear, and despair.

At Low Torning, for example, Ged's reentry into Earthsea society is fortunately eased by the boatmaker Pechvarry, who offers Ged friendship; Ged weaves some protective spells for Pechvarry's boats and Pechvarry gives Ged sailing lessons. The exchange of gifts is a manifestation of the trust that makes human community possible; Ged's participation in the act testifies to his growing awareness of his social role. Conversely, Ged witnesses the betrayal in human society when he finds the old couple on the desert island; he sees the consequences, this time in the political sphere, of misused power.

Ged learns of the reality of death and of evil in the

world. When he gives in to the temptation to bring Pechvarry's son back from the land of the dead and when he faces the temptation of the Terrenon, Ged learns that neither death nor evil can be eliminated, but that he is free to choose how he deals with each. He chooses to stop denying death and chooses not to serve evil.

In rejecting the power and information which Terrenon and the dragon Yevaud offer Ged, he is choosing to protect the human community and the Equilibrium rather than enhance his own power. Le Guin's dragon, more Oriental than Occidental, seems to be an archetype for the forces of nature which are powerful and wise, yet neither malevolent nor benevolent toward humankind. Ged earns the title "dragonlord" not because he slays the dragon but because he converses with it; he accepts its coexistence with humankind. Likewise, he accepts the wisdom of the silent, less obtrusive elements of nature, such as the otak.

In his schooling with Ogion and on Roke, Ged's arrogance kept him from hearing the truth in his mentors' lessons. However, after experiencing despair, death, the temptations for increased power, Ged can finally listen to advice. Seeking home and Ogion, his mentor-father who named him, Ged is counseled to "turn clear round, and seek the very source, and that which lies before the source. There lies your hope of strength" (128). Ged learns that the most important knowledge is of one's being ("the source") and one's

beginning ("that which lies before the source"), the realities of his own psyche. The shadow acts out of the
very power that Ged has refused to recognize in himself, primarily the desire to control.

In the recognition scene which is also the climax of
the novel, Ged meets the shadow for the last time. They
lay hold of each other and speak the same name, "Ged."
Light and shadow mingle, and there are no longer two
beings but only one. Ged has acknowledged the dark
side of his self, such characteristics as arrogance, ignorance, fear of death, the desire to control and to master.
His friend and fellow sorcerer, Vetch, understands the
significance of the act:

that Ged had neither lost nor won but, naming the
shadow of his death with his own name, had made
himself whole: a man: who, knowing his whole true
self, cannot be used or possessed by any power other
than himself, and whose life therefore is lived for life's
sake and never in the service of ruin, or pain, or hatred,
or the dark (180–81).

Ged has acknowledged the presence of good and evil
in himself and transformed himself psychologically to
fit into the world. He has learned through experience
what his mages and masters sought to teach him at
Roke, that a wizard's power "must follow knowledge,
and serve need" (44). He must act out of knowledge of
the myriad powers and must act only when there is

a clear need to assist the Equilibrium or the human community. To participate, not to change; to act appropriately, not to master—these become Ged's ethical principles.

"To light a candle is to cast a shadow" brings together the imagery of the novel and the lessons Ged has learned. He must proceed with caution, for uncertainty is perhaps the one certain thing he knows about the world; an increase in knowledge (light) is accompanied by the realization of further ignorance. Furthermore, every act ("to light") has consequences for which the actor is responsible; all existence is interconnected; therefore, the individual must exercise freedom carefully. Apparent opposites such as light and dark are actually complementarities; knowledge of one leads to knowledge of the other, and one must learn to cope with their presence—life and death, good and evil, pleasure and pain. The central imagery is used in the five-line poem which begins the novel:

> Only in silence the word,
> only in dark the light,
> only in dying life:
> bright the hawk's flight
> on the empty sky.

Life is accompanied by mortality ("empty sky"); knowledge of one's vulnerability and brevity gives one the opportunity to act meaningfully.

The novel ends with the successful completion of

Ged's journey into himself and his attainment of adult-hood. Ged's journey, which can be traced on Le Guin's map of Earthsea in the novel, is in the pattern of an unclosed circle or spiral. The pattern, seen in other Le Guin novels, suggests that a journey into the self does not end with the return to the beginning place. The successful completion of the journey means the hero has been changed. Further, the unfinished circle, coming at the end of the novel, suggests that one's life is a series of changes or transformations. Thus, although the novel began as a single volume and has a sense of an ending, its image of the open circle suggests the possibility of further narratives.

In *The Tombs of Atuan* Le Guin examines the coming-of-age story under different circumstances. The protagonist is a young woman, Tenar, and she lives on the margin rather than at the center of Earthsea. Second, unlike Ged, whose development was a result of his own choices, Tenar has had an identity forced upon her just as surely as her black clothing has been woven and put upon her. Further, Tenar's acts and eventual quest are more public than Ged's. Ged's quest was private, a confrontation with the realities of his psyche. Tenar's decisions, however, have immediate sociopolitical consequences. *A Wizard of Earthsea* focused on the journey inward to knowledge of the self; *The Tombs of Atuan* focuses on the journey outward to knowledge of the relationship between self and human community.

Le Guin again uses the omniscient point of view for

the narrative, but she lets *A Wizard of Earthsea* establish the context for the second novel. Ged appears as a character midway in the novel; the crisis is caused by the threat to the Equilibrium's balance by the Dark Powers and the threat to Earthsea's political harmony by the Kargad Empire.

Both of these powers are preventing Tenar's normal psychological development into selfhood and womanhood. This active opposition to Tenar's coming of age places Le Guin's novel in the tradition of the female *Bildungsroman*. Annis Pratt, in her study *Archetypal Patterns in Women's Fiction*, writes of this tradition:

The novel of development portrays a world in which the young woman hero is destined for disappointment. The vitality and hopefulness characterizing the adolescent hero's attitude toward her future here meet and conflict with the expectations and dictates of the surrounding society. Every element of her desired world— freedom to come and go, allegiance to nature, meaningful work, exercise of the intellect, and use of her own erotic capabilities—inevitably clashes with patriarchal norms.[21]

What the adolescent needs for her development into an adult is not what society needs her to have. The adolescent woman experiences, Pratt writes, a "collision between the hero's evolving self and society's imposed identity."[22] *The Tombs of Atuan* and other similar

EARTHSEA

stories use images of suffocation, entrapment, and madness to portray the woman's plight. By contrast, the male *Bildungsroman* usually shows the adolescent achieving the characteristics of an adult which are those society needs him to have, as illustrated in *A Wizard of Earthsea*. By setting Tenar's struggle in the Kargad Empire, Le Guin can portray Tenar's rebellion against the patriarchal empire and then have her escape into a different society where she will have the freedom to define herself and to learn to choose and act responsibly.

The Kargad Empire (the four islands of Atuan, Karego-At, Atnini, and Hur-at-Hur) is a theocracy; its divine monarch, the Godking, claims to be the human representative of the Nameless Ones, sometimes called the Dark Powers. Older than the human race, they are the "powers of the dark, of ruin, of madness";[23] their greatest stronghold is in the desert on the island of Atuan, where they dwell in a below-ground labyrinth. On this site are ancient Kargish temples to the Godkings and to the Dark Powers. Rejecting the concept of the Equilibrium, the Godkings' primary interests are keeping the empire together and keeping themselves in power; their society is militant and patriarchal. It is doubtful whether the kings and aristocracy even believe in the Dark Powers any longer; but the leaders need a symbol of their power base, particularly they need the One Priestess as a figurehead. The child chosen to become the Priestess is, then, their ultimate human sacrifice, symbolic of their devotion to destruction.

The Tombs of Atuan tells the story of this titular head of the Kargish religion. As part of her initiation she is given a new name (Arha, which means "the Eaten One") and, as her special domain, a man-made underground labyrinth which has "no beginning, and no end . . . no center" (68). Tenar is trapped. Psychologically her development is arrested between being a child and becoming a woman. Politically she is trapped into carrying out the bidding of the monarch and his religious representative at Atuan, although ostensibly she holds the position of supreme power. Socially she is trapped in the identity of the One Priestess; she is "the new body of the Priestess who died" (10). Tenar's knowledge is as narrow as the dark labyrinth which she paces and memorizes. Like Ged in *A Wizard of Earthsea* she must "turn clear round," see into herself, and so be forever changed. It is a mistake to say that Ged "saves" Tenar; she saves herself, but Ged functions as the midwife in her rebirth.

Le Guin once wrote that the subject of *The Tombs of Atuan* was sex, by which she apparently meant not only the physical maturity but also the recognition of and potential for intimate interaction with that which is different. Rollo May identified such maturation as *eros*; his definition is helpful in describing what Tenar must learn:

a desiring, longing, a forever reaching out, seeking to expand . . . the drive toward union with significant other persons in our world in relation to whom we discover our own self-fulfillment. Eros is the yearning in man which leads him to dedicate himself to seeking *arête*, the noble and good life.[24]

The Place mirrors female experience in Kargish society. Ostensibly protected by its walls and guards and eunuchs, the women are actually imprisoned. Ostensibly honored by their society, they are actually punished by being isolated, perhaps a reflection of the male fear of the female principle. Ostensibly powerful in their roles as religious leaders, they are actually functionaries who have internalized male standards and enforce them. The women have become their own prison guards, figuratively speaking. Kossil is the epitome of the woman who is imprisoned and imprisoning; she is cruel, hateful, unable to nurture anyone, obsessed with the desire for power.

The labyrinth symbolizes the women's imprisonment. Deep underground, changeless and dark, it is a closed circle; one door leads in but not out, and the other door leads in and then out into the Temple of the Nameless Ones. It is a tomb for the meaningful lives these women might have led and for the kind of society Kargad could have become. The labyrinth also symbolizes Arha, the dark side of Tenar's self; her passage into adulthood must involve a confrontation with the light just as traumatic as was Ged's confrontation with the dark. The extent of her darkness is evident in her thinking of the labyrinth as a "safe" place (57) and in her choosing to spend hours exploring it. She becomes a good priestess by choosing to repress rather than to explore her self. Although there are many hints that Arha is not completely satisfied with her life at the Place, it is not until she must deal with her first political prisoners that she begins the self-struggle toward rebirth.

When Tenar kills the three political prisoners, she has become like Kossil. However, her illness and nightmares suggest that her entire self was not "eaten" when she was consecrated as the One Priestess. Her respect for life finds expression through her unconscious. During her recovery a conversation with Penthe makes Tenar conscious of different knowledge of the world. Penthe rejects the divinity of the Atuan monarch, and although Arha is initially shocked by this "unfaith," she begins to see the world differently: "she felt as if she had looked up and suddenly seen a whole new planet hanging huge and populous right outside the window, an entirely strange world, one in which the gods did not matter" (41).

The stimulus which leads to Arha's new sense of self, however, is Ged, who comes into the labyrinth searching for the missing half of the Ring of Erreth-Akbe. Ged's presence and his knowledge contradict what Arha knows about herself, the empire, other Earthsea people, and the powers of darkness. Ged is wholly different from her in sex, skin color, place of origin, religion. The symbol of his otherness is light; his wizardly staff lights the Undertomb and she sees, for the first time in her life, its beauty. To suddenly find light in the place of darkness, life instead of death, beauty instead of blackness, shocks her.

But her own actions also begin to shock her. To continue to keep Ged alive in the labyrinth is to defy all her religious teachings and to defy the evil powers she serves. To sacrifice him is to defy her respect for life and her need to know more about the world, about the other. This dilemma is a classic battle between the social persona and the real self. All that she needs and desires to become an adult woman clashes with what the god-kings need her to be—obedient and dependent.

Nearly one-third of the novel details Arha's dilemma as she painfully tries to turn clear around to encounter her repressed self or, just as painfully, tries to deny the new knowledge that Ged has brought to light. After Ged calls her by the name her parents gave her, she confronts her dual selves, and she dreams of struggling in a grave in which she has been buried alive. Such an image of suffocation is common in the female *Bildungsroman,* as is her approach to madness when she cries out alternately, "I am Tenar" (96), "Who am I?" (99), "I am not Tenar. I am not Arha" (104). At this turning point of her life Ged clarifies her choices: she must either sacrifice him and resume her identity as Arha, or she must "unlock the door" and become Tenar in the larger world of Earthsea.

At their last meeting in the Treasure Room they exchange gifts, a manifestation of the bond between them, that which makes possible human community. Its essential elements are nurturance, trust, cooperation, respect for the other. The symbol of the bond is the rejoined ring; it reveals the Bond-Rune needed by a king to bring unity to Earthsea. Tenar's rune, then, symbolizes unity; the ring, Tenar's self, the islands of Earthsea are all joined.

Together, with Ged's magery to hold off the Dark Powers and with Tenar's knowledge of the labyrinth, they escape Ged's physical grave and Tenar's psychological one. Tenar's release is imaged as a birth, and Ged assists her like a midwife, appealing to her sense of commitment and responsibility and to her true being to perform the act that is a natural step in her maturation. Wearing the bond-ring, she steps out. As they flee, the Nameless Ones level the Place in an earthquake; their anger destroys themselves, the same fate that had awaited Arha.

Tenar now begins the physical journey that represents her coming of age, and the novel ends with that journey barely started. She is so scarred by her belief in the powers of destruction and has so little knowledge of the outside world that she contemplates extreme acts of murder and martyrdom. That she would think of these as solutions indicates how strongly the powers of darkness hold her. Her desire to kill Ged is a desire to destroy the other which she momentarily blames for her own pain. Her desire for martyrdom is equally destructive. What she must accept, as Ged helps her to realize, is her guilt. She has done evil; she did not choose to serve the evil, but she can now choose not to. She learns that: "freedom is a heavy load, a great and strange burden for the spirit to undertake. It is not easy. It is not a gift given, but a choice made, and the choice may be a hard one. The road goes upward towards the light; but the laden traveler may never reach the end of it" (141).

Just as Ged will always have the physical scars of his battle with his shadow, so Tenar will always have the psychological scars of her battle with external and internal evil. Ged's image of her vulnerability, consistent with the novel's light-and-dark imagery, is of a newly lit lamp which needs to "burn out of the wind awhile" (145). From Ged's suggestions at the end of this novel and brief references in *The Farthest Shore* the reader knows that Tenar went to Gont, to continue her healing under the care of Ogion, and that she became known and honored throughout Earthsea as the White Lady of Gont, Tenar of the Ring. Le Guin has thus provided a glimpse of a life which continues to be heroic. Having given birth to herself, destroyed the power base of the Kargad Empire and its official religion, and restored the ring of unity to Earthsea, Tenar chooses the independent life which will allow her the freedom to continue to define herself and to learn about the world.

Tenar is actually more of a revolutionist than either Ged or Arren. She has had to rebel against and break free of the society that nurtured her; Ged and Arren mature so as to fit into their home societies. Thus, "coming home," the image on both the first and last pages of the novel, is problematic for her. Although the people of Havnor welcome her, she chooses a less populated place—the mountains of Gont with Ogion. She will have one of the most celebrated mages in Earthsea as her teacher, the only man who could cure Ged when he stayed too long in the shape of a hawk. Tenar, at fifteen, has been trapped too long in the shape of the One Priestess of the Nameless Ones. Further, she will be connected to the world of nature on Gont, to the cycles of death and rebirth in the seasons of the year.

Tenar's new knowledge that brings her across the threshold of adulthood is, like Ged's, knowledge of power. On the broadest level she has learned that the cosmos is not under the sole influence of the power of darkness but of the power of light, too. Ged's lesson on the nature of these balanced powers is clear: The Dark Powers

should not be denied nor forgotten, but neither should they be worshiped. The Earth is beautiful, and bright, and kindly, but that is not all. The Earth is also terrible, and dark, and cruel. The rabbit shrieks dying in the green meadows. The mountains clench their great hands full of hidden fire. There are sharks in the sea, and there is cruelty in men's eyes. And where men

worship these things and abase themselves before
them, there evil breeds (106–07).

She also begins to put the power of the empire into
perspective. In contrast to Earthsea, Kargad is small and
destructive. On the personal level she learns that her
own power is not that which she was given as the rein-
carnated priestess, but that which she acquired in
choosing to leave the labyrinth. It is the power of dealing with the other, making choices for herself, and accepting the consequences of her choices. Power on all
these levels, Tenar learns, is not only force, mastery,
authority, and enslavement; power is also cooperation,
trust, creating new relationships, acting within the network of the human and cosmic community. Because
acknowledgment of the other is so crucial to Tenar's
successful transition from adolescent to adult, she can
be thought of as the spirit of human community; she
has achieved bonding through both love and pain, gain
and loss.

The coming-of-age story which Le Guin tells in *The
Farthest Shore* is more like Ged's than Tenar's. Not only
is the adolescent again a male, but the process is symbolized by a spiral journey out to distant islands, across
open sea, and back to the Inner Lands. Furthermore,
Arren is not trapped in an identity as Tenar was. However, like Tenar he has no wizardly powers; his power,
he must discover, is the ability to lead and to govern.

The novel presents yet a third variation of the coming-of-age narrative; it is the story of the hero who is tested before he becomes king. The adolescent hero, Arren, born into the oldest royal house, has the potential to become the king for which the people of Earthsea have been waiting eight hundred years. The sequence of events is close to the paradigm of the testing of the mythic hero. For example, using the Greek stories Northrop Frye lists seven features of the paradigm: "Mysterious birth, oracular prophecies about the future contortions of the plot, foster parents, adventures which involve capture by pirates, narrow escapes from death, recognition of the true identity of the hero and his eventual marriage with the heroine."[25] Le Guin includes all but the first and the last in her account of several months in Arren's life.

Of greater importance, however, are two other differences between this novel and the previous two. First, the consequences of the characters' actions are shown in the largest political context. In the novel the Dark Mage has broken the Equilibrium, is turning all of Earthsea into a wasteland, and has challenged the authority of both Roke and Havnor. Second, the success of this quest depends on the bond relationship of Ged and Arren. Arren and Ged begin and end a long journey together; and Arren moves from a naïve, unquestioned fealty to Ged, through despair and alienation from him, to a mature acceptance of himself and Ged. The final act of fealty is that which Ged swears to Arren, the long-awaited King of Earthsea.

Although Le Guin shows Arren's courage and heroism, as one would expect in a traditional account of the testing of the hero-king, she examines in detail the process by which these traits are acquired. To discuss the stages of Arren's transformation the language of anthropology is especially helpful. Noting analogues in literature and myth and history, Victor Turner has projected the three stages of the initiation rites in African tribes into all social situations of transition. These three stages are "separation, margin (or *limen*, signifying 'threshold' in Latin), and aggregation." He briefly defines them as follows:

The first phase (of separation) comprises symbolic behavior signifying the detachment of the individual or group either from an earlier fixed point in the social structure, from a set of cultural conditions (a "state"), or from both. During the intervening "liminal" period, the characteristics of the ritual subject (the "passenger") are ambiguous; he passes through a cultural realm that has few or none of the attributes of the past or coming state. In the third phase (reaggregation or reincorporation), the passage is consummated. The ritual subject, individual or corporate, is in a relatively stable state once more and, by virtue of this . . . he is expected to behave in accordance with certain customary norms and ethical standards binding on incumbents of social position in a system of such positions.[26]

In the opening three chapters Le Guin shows that Arren and Ged are aware that they are considering a significant separation from homeland, known associates, and social roles. Arren offers to accompany Ged, and Ged chooses him as a "fit companion," acknowledging that he "never needed help before."[27] Arren's initial concern is that he will fail Ged. Upon leaving Roke in Ged's sailboat *Lookfar*, they begin "an unsafe journey to an unknown end" (28) by entering liminality, the second phase of the physical and psychological journey.

On their journey, cut off from associates and the need to function in their customary roles, Arren has only Ged as a representative of human community. The social bond, the most elemental feature which makes human society possible, is what Turner calls *communitas*, a "communion of equal individuals,"[28] a bonding outside of the structured sociopolitical system. Arren's coming of age is a journey toward both understanding the bond of trust and fealty with the other and understanding himself, for unless he "turns clear round" and looks at the very desires he tries to repress, he cannot have a mature, honest relationship with the other.

Arren tries to repress his desire for immortality. Like Tenar, however, his dreams and nightmares pressure him toward self-awareness. Just as Tenar dreamed of suffocating when she felt the pressure to be Arha, so Arren dreams of being chained or being wrapped in cobwebs when he feels the pressure to deny the dark side of himself. That Arren is tempted by the desire for immortality is first revealed in Hort Town. While Ged tries to stay with Hare in his trance, Arren suddenly breaks through to that which Hare seeks: "There, in the vast, dry darkness, there one stood beckoning. *Come,* he said, the tall lord of shadows. In his hand he held a tiny flame no larger than a pearl, held it out to Arren, offering life. Slowly Arren took one step toward him, following" (54–55).

This step is as much a step into adulthood as was the step Arren took to get into Ged's boat and begin the journey. No longer functioning as the dependent child to father-Ged, he steps out toward something he wants. It is a step toward that which he must admit and confront, the dark side of himself, his potential for evil—in this case his desire for something which violates nature.

When Arren represses thoughts of his desires, his dreams are affected. Although the dreams foreshadow his experience in the land of death, they also suggest Arren's powerlessness as long as he continues to deny his own potential for evil. The fear and repression are intensified by Sopli's presence; his fears of death and desire for immortality echo Arren's inmost thoughts. When Ged is wounded, Arren is so overcome with the presence and fear of death that he cannot think or act. Unwilling to examine himself, he blames Ged for all that has happened; despairing, he sees Ged with "no power left in him, no wizardry, no strength, not even youth, nothing" (108). Having denied his own potential for evil, he has essentially been fostering and believing in a false self; when it crumbles, there is nothing for Arren to get hold of to help him solve the problems. He is without hope.

Rescued from near death by the raft people, Arren recovers as he reestablishes the bond of trust and love with Ged and as he thinks critically about the social bond of the raft people. Arren confronts his dishonesty about himself and about his bond with the other when he courageously confesses to Ged the depths of his despair. The ensuing conversation is similar to those between Ogion and Ged when Ogion told Ged he must look into himself, and between Ged and Tenar when Ged told her what her name was. In all three psychological healing begins when the problem and solution can be named, when the admission of weakness becomes strength. The society of the raft people challenges the idea of a commitment to the larger society of Earthsea. In contrast to the chief's refusal to accept any responsibility for that larger society, Arren includes the raft people in his commitment, as indicated when he sings in the dawn and celebrates the creation of all of Earthsea.

In addition to this new knowledge about himself and society Arren also learns more about his participation in the Equilibrium. This interdependence of nature and humans is represented in the reciprocal relationship of dragon and man. In Earthsea, instead of suggesting the destructiveness of nature, Le Guin's dragon suggests the ancient, wise, enigmatic aspect of nature which will always be different from human life but affected by it.

Arren's experiences in the land of the dead strengthen his commitments. He encounters the dead who have lost themselves and the *communitas* bond with others. Void of reason, feeling, and the art of making anything, they are the shells of people once living; Arren has thus come to knowledge of the death he feared, and it no longer frightens him. Arren also discerns that Cob has lost his selfhood and *communitas.* Unable to experience love, he exists in isolation and alienation; existence has been reduced to the struggle for power. Symbolically, Cob's eye sockets are empty; he has sacrificed his self ("I"), his ability to see the power of light, his ability to see the natural environment and human community. Rejecting Cob's offer of immortality, Arren leads Ged to Cob so that Ged can restore the wholeness of the world.

Arren continues to be the leader as he chooses their way out to the shores of light. Crossing the mountains of pain symbolizes Arren's acceptance of pain and mortality as elements of the personal, social, and cosmic life he has come to understand. Their return to Roke on the back of the oldest dragon is dramatic, partly because this cooperation between human and nonhuman symbolizes the balance of apparent opposites that Ged and Arren have restored to Earthsea which makes possible the Equilibrium, the kingdom of Earthsea, and the integrated self. Ged kneels to Arren, acknowledging his acceptance of him as the next king of Earthsea and symbolizing the irrevocable changes which occurred for both of them in liminality.

Life Story of the Wizard

Each volume of the Earthsea trilogy tells a different story about the coming-of-age process. When viewed together, the completed trilogy provides Ged's life history, which is both a story of the epic hero who successfully deals with the forces that threaten the Equilibrium and the kingdom and a story of the epic hero as creative artist.

Each of the novels recounts a quest at a different stage in Ged's life. As a youth he hunted down the shadow which he released into the world; as a mature wizard he searched for the missing half of the Ring of Erreth-Akbe whose Bond-Rune ensures the king's successful reign; and as an old man he tracked Cob, who opened a hole in the world and returned from the dead. Scholars have applied a number of different structures to his life story. Following Joseph Campbell's analysis of the archetypal journey in *The Hero with a Thousand Faces,* Virginia White sees a "pattern of departure, initiation, and return" in the three quests. Following

Jung's analysis of the psychological journey, Margaret P. Esmonde identifies the story as "a progression of an ego from uncertainty and self-doubt to assurance and fulfillment." Charlotte Spivack summarizes the life as being the "paradigmatic career of the mythic hero . . . ; the divine signs of talent . . . [in] childhood, . . . trial and quest, periods of meditation and withdrawal, symbolic death and journey to the underworld, and, finally, rebirth and apotheosis."[29]

Le Guin has emphasized the psychological qualities of the story in her selection of the key events of Ged's life to narrate. The reader learns, for example, that Ged's most famous deeds are not featured in the three novels. Instead of focusing on the public deeds, the deeds that ensured his sociopolitical role in external society, Le Guin examines the deeds which show Ged's inner struggles and psychological growth. After all, as Ged tells Arren in *The Farthest Shore*, heroes are "the ones who seek to be themselves" (135).

As the life story of a wizard, the trilogy is also a story of the efficacy of art. In "Dreams Must Explain Themselves," Le Guin discusses this meaning:

I said that to know the true name is to know the thing, for me, and for the wizards. This implies a good deal about the "meaning" of the trilogy, and about me. The trilogy is, in one aspect, about the artist. The artist as magician. The Trickster. Prospero. That is the only truly allegorical aspect it has of which I am conscious. . . .

Wizardry is artistry. The trilogy is then, in this sense, about art, the creative experience, the creative process. There is always this circularity in fantasy. The snake devours its tail. Dreams must explain themselves.[30]

Ged should not be regarded as a disguised Le Guin; he is more like a muse for her, a model for the artist to aspire to. Le Guin has called him her guide in Earthsea. The magic of Earthsea, sometimes called "artmagic," depends, as does fiction, on the user's genius and knowledge of language. Like the work of art, the magic transforms reality. Patricia Dooley summarized the correspondences among magic, art, and the world: "Magic becomes a sophisticated metaphor for the ability of art to influence the experiential world through the insubstantial medium of the imagination."[31] The magician, trickster, and Prospero are all creator-destroyers who shock and delight and edify.

Just as the life of the epic hero is developed in stages from youth to old age, so the trilogy also depicts the life of the artist-wizard progressively from youth to maturity. In *A Wizard of Earthsea* Ged becomes aware of his innate power and learns from his masters, as an artist learns from mentors, how to discipline it. Discipline of the imagination, Le Guin has written, "does not mean to repress it, but to train it—to encourage it to grow, and act, and be fruitful."[32] Like Ged, the artist must have a fully developed knowledge of the self and will, in fact, find the journey into the self a creative

connection between the conscious and the collective unconscious. Le Guin writes: "To reach the others, the
artist goes into himself. Using reason, he deliberately
enters the irrational. The farther he goes into himself,
the closer he comes to the other."[33] Ged learns to resist
the easy roads to knowledge and power, the route of a
Faustus or a formula novelist who barters away power
or talent.

The artist-wizard, once sure of his talent, begins a
lifelong search for names, the "right words," by which
he exercises his power. "For me," Le Guin wrote, "as
for the wizards, to know the name of an island or a
character is to know the island or the person. Usually
the name comes of itself, but sometimes one must be
very careful: as I was with the protagonist, whose true
name is Ged."[34] In general, the power of language for
the writer comes from the idea that if a thing can be
named (be it an object, a theory, a tool, a psychological
trait), then its existence can be dealt with, can be made
a part of the reader's experience. The threat of the dragons of Pendor is solved when Ged can call Yevaud by its
name; the threat of the shadow, of all that Ged fears and
represses, is absolved into an acknowledged part of
himself when he can name it, Ged. More specifically,
in Le Guin's philosophy of life, the power of naming
also lies in its ability to honor the thing which is being
named. As T. A. Shippey has argued, Le Guin's emphasis on the word "is bound up with an attitude of respect
for all parts of creation (even rocks), and a wary reluc-

tance to operate on any of them without a total awareness of their distinct and individual nature."[35] Shippey
asserts that Le Guin thus critiques the modern attitudes
of materialism and industrialization, which are anthro-
pocentric. Shippey states that Le Guin puts the word
above the thing, but it is more accurate to say that Le
Guin regards them as equal.

A Wizard of Earthsea can be regarded as depicting
the artist in apprenticeship, and *The Tombs of Atuan* depicts the mature artist confronting a hostile audience
and gradually transforming that person's perception of
reality. What Ged tells Tenar about the world outside
the Place and the Kargad Empire is, to her, fiction in the
sense that it is a very different world and one which she
has never experienced. Her hostility toward his art is
based on her false education and on fear. She is a dis-
believer and sneers at his art as mere illusion. Le Guin
wrote of such a hostile audience in "Why Are Americans Afraid of Dragons?" where she identified the
"hardworking, over-thirty American male" in business
as one who dismisses fiction, especially fantasy, because he has learned to repress his imagination.[36] Ged
assists Tenar by showing her beauty, joy, and light; he
assists her by the words which reveal a larger, more
humane world and by the word for her other self,
Tenar.

The Farthest Shore depicts the artist toward the end
of his life, assisting an entire country in dealing with a
crisis of language. His action for the prince, the king-

born, is the same as that for Tenar; he gives assistance, offers stories of another kind of existence and a different system of values, and then allows the young prince to choose. All of Earthsea is threatened by the disbelief in artmagic; wizards are forgetting the true names of things and are losing their own true names, dragons lose the power of speech. The artist in his old age is the only one who can reestablish balance because, as Ged says of himself, "I desire nothing beyond my art" (133). He is not vulnerable to temptation.

Ged's belief that there is no escape from death is carried to its logical extension when he retires at the end of *The Farthest Shore*. Powerful as artistry is, it cannot provide a permanent escape to another world. Artist and reader alike must also deal with the consensus reality which surrounds them and with the limits of time and power. No artist's power is permanent, and one who is tempted to believe that it is goes the way of Cob or Faustus. No artist's role as aesthetic and moral guide for the people is permanent. An artist, Le Guin suggests in this novel, may uphold the standards when the ruling powers are deficient, but such is not the permanent role of the artist. Le Guin is conscious of her own lapses into didacticism, i.e., when the message overpowers the story, when the artist begins "to preach" rather than allowing people the freedom they need to be transformed.[37] So the trilogy ends with news of the coronation of Arren as King of Earthsea, and the reader's attention is focused on the social realm. Ged retires, satisfied and fulfilled. Given the difficulty with which he has learned the lesson of turning clear around, of always seeking to connect with his roots in his actions, the ending is—like all of his quest journeys—an open circle. He returns to his beginning, to Roke and to the life of contemplation which he had rejected as a young man. But he returns as a changed man. The creative process has also transformed the artist.

Notes

1. Le Guin, "Dreams Must Explain Themselves," *The Language of the Night*, ed. Susan Wood (New York: Putnam's, 1979) 55.

2. Le Guin, "The Child and the Shadow," *Language of the Night* 65.

3. "The Child and the Shadow" 63.

4. "The Child and the Shadow" 65.

5. "The Child and the Shadow" 70.

6. Francis J. Molson, "The Earthsea Trilogy: Ethical Fantasy for Children," *Ursula K. Le Guin: Voyager to Inner Lands and to Outer Space*, ed. Joe De Bolt (Port Washington, NY: Kennikat, 1979), 130.

7. Nicholas O'Connell, "Ursula K. Le Guin," *At the Field's End: Interviews with Twenty Pacific Northwest Writers* (Seattle: Madrona, 1987) 28.

8. "Dreams Must Explain Themselves" 53.

9. "Dreams Must Explain Themselves" 50.

10. Le Guin *The Farthest Shore* (New York: Bantam, 1975) 128, 15.

11. Werner Heisenberg, "The Representation of Nature in Contemporary Physics," *The Discontinuous Universe*, ed. Sallie Sears and Georgianna W. Lord (New York: Basic Books, 1972) 134.

12. *The Farthest Shore* 66.

13. *The Farthest Shore* 17.

14. Margaret P. Esmonde, "The Master Pattern: The Psychological Journey in the Earthsea Trilogy," *Ursula K. Le Guin*, ed. Joseph D. Olander and Martin Harry Greenberg (New York: Taplinger, 1979) 15–35, 225.

15. Richard F. Patteson, "Le Guin's Earthsea Trilogy: The Psychology of Fantasy," *The Scope of the Fantastic*, ed. Robert A. Collins and Howard D. Pearce (Westport, CT: Greenwood, 1985) 240.

16. Le Guin, "A Response to the Le Guin Issue," *Science-Fiction Studies* 3 (1976): 45. See also Thomas J. Remington and Robert Galbreath, "Lagniappe: An Informal Dialogue with Ursula K. Le Guin," *Selected Proceedings of the 1978 Science Fiction Research Association National Conference* (Cedar Falls: University of Northern Iowa, 1979) 270–71.

17. Le Guin, "A Citizen of Mondath," *Language of the Night* 25; Remington and Galbreath 271.

18. Le Guin, *A Wizard of Earthsea* (New York: Bantam, 1975) 16. Subsequent references will be noted in parentheses.

19. "The Child and the Shadow" 66–67. Two of Le Guin's own sources on Taoism are Holmes Welch, *Taoism: The Parting of the Way* (Boston: Beacon Press, 1966), and Joseph Needham, *Science and Civilisation in China*, vol. 2 (Cambridge: Cambridge University Press, 1962).

20. "The Child and the Shadow" 64.

21. Annis Pratt, *Archetypal Patterns in Women's Fiction* (Bloomimgton: Indiana University Press, 1981) 29.

22. Pratt 29.

23. Le Guin, *The Tombs of Atuan* (New York: Bantam, 1975) 107. Subsequent references will be noted in parentheses.

24. Rollo May, *Love and Will* (New York: Norton, 1969) 73–74; quoted Pratt 74.

25. Northrop Frye, *The Secular Scripture* (Cambridge, MA: Harvard University Press, 1976) 4.

26. Victor Turner, *The Ritual Process: Structure and Anti-Structure* (Ithaca: Cornell University Press, 1969) 94–95.

27. *The Farthest Shore* 25. Subsequent references will be noted in parentheses.

28. Turner 96.

29. Virginia White, "Bright the Hawk's Flight: The Journey of the Hero in Ursula Le Guin's Earthsea Trilogy," *Ball State University Forum* 20 (1979) 34; Esmonde 16; Charlotte Spivack, *Ursula K. Le Guin* (Boston: Twayne, 1984) 42.

30. "Dreams Must Explain Themselves" 53.

31. Patricia Dooley, "Magic and Art in Ursula Le Guin's Earthsea Trilogy," *Children's Literature* (New Haven: Yale University Press) 8: 103.

32. Le Guin, "Why Are Americans Afraid of Dragons," *Language of the Night* 41.

33. Le Guin, "Myth and Archetype in Science Fiction," *Language of the Night* 78.

34. "Dreams Must Explain Themselves" 52.

35. T. A. Shippey, "The Magic Art and the Evolution of Words: Ursula Le Guin's Earthsea Trilogy," *Mosaic* 10 (1977): 152.

36. "Why Are Americans Afraid of Dragons?" 40.

37. "Introduction to *The Word for World is Forest*," *Language of the Night* 151.

CHAPTER THREE

The Hainish World

Where Le Guin's fantasy novels place the psychological journey of discovery on a mystical background called the Equilibrium, her science fiction works place the journey in sociopolitical settings which have some affinity with consensus reality. Le Guin has commented that "the unique aesthetic delight of SF [lies] in the intense, coherent following-through of the implications of an idea, whether it's a bit of far-out technology, or a theory in quantum mechanics, or a satirical projection of current social trends, or a whole world created by extrapolating from biology and ethnology."[1]

Science fiction connects with the reader's sense of reality because its authors derive their alternate worlds from supposing a radical difference from some existing area of knowledge. The invention or extrapolation also distances the reader from the people and events in consensus reality. Distanced from one's own world, yet still connected to it in time or space, the reader confronts "anew" the old world. Science fiction, as the commonplace saying goes, is about the here and now.

UNDERSTANDING URSULA K. LE GUIN

Le Guin shares with most other science fiction writers the belief that this type of writing has a unique place in modern literature. Often quoted is Le Guin's analogy of science and science fiction as an open house:

If science fiction has a major gift to offer literature, I think it is just this: the capacity to face an open universe. Physically open, psychically open. No doors shut.

What science, from physics and astronomy to history and psychology, has given us is the open universe: a cosmos that is not a simple, fixed hierarchy, but an immensely complex process in time. All the doors stand open, from the prehuman past through the incredible present to the terrible and hopeful future. All connections are possible. All alternatives are thinkable. It is not a comfortable, reassuring place. It's a very large house, a very drafty house. But it's the house we live in.[2]

In constructing her science fiction worlds Le Guin uses the scientist's technique of the thought experiment. In her 1976 introduction to *The Left Hand of Darkness* she wrote: "The purpose of a thought-experiment, as the term was used by Schrödinger and other physicists, is not to predict the future—indeed Schrödinger's most famous thought-experiment goes to show that the 'future,' on the quantum level, *cannot* be predicted—but to describe reality, the present world."[3]

Le Guin finds that the thought experiment results

THE HAINISH WORLD

in a more complex novel than the technique of extrapolation. Extrapolation predicts what will occur in the future on the basis of what is being done in the present; Le Guin argues it is "too rationalist and simplistic." It uses too few variables and its starting point is, "If this goes on, this is what will happen." The thought experiment, on the other hand, follows a more open kind of thinking: "Let's say this or that is such and so, and see what happens."[4] The thought experiment, she argues, gets at some truths about "this world, ourselves, the way we go."[5] Another advantage of this technique is that "thought and intuition can move freely within bounds set only by the terms of the experiment, which may be very large indeed."[6] Le Guin uses two thought experiments for each novel set in the Hainish world. In the background is the idea of a common origin, loss of contact, and reunification for all the planets; and in the foreground is the idea which is unique to each novel.

Le Guin's thought experiment for the common background of the Hainish novels could be reconstructed thus: Let's say that a million or a half-million years ago intelligent humanoids from the planet Hain established different varieties of their race on the habitable planets. Let's also say that after losing contact for many centuries, the Hainish began to revisit the planets (approximately during Earth's twenty-first century). Now, let's see what happens. The terms of the Hainish experiment are minimal. Why the Hainish carried out the seeding project is unknown, although some of the nearly one hundred planets, specifically Earth and Gethen, seem to have been biological experiments. Le Guin never states what events led to the planets' losing or resuming contact, but in both *The Left Hand of Darkness* and *The Dispossessed* a character speculates about the ancient race and wonders if they were motivated by guilt for "treating lives as things."[7]

Using the Hainish world, Le Guin published six novels and four short stories from 1964 to 1974: "The Dowry of Angyar" (1964), *Rocannon's World* (1966), *Planet of Exile* (1966), *City of Illusions* (1967), "Winter's King" (1969), *The Left Hand of Darkness* (1969), *The Word for World is Forest* (1972), "Vaster than Empires and More Slow" (1971), *The Dispossessed* (1974), "The Day Before the Revolution" (1974). Both internal and external evidence indicates that Le Guin did not begin with all the details of the world worked out but rather shaped it as she went along.[8] Her first publications depict events in the far future, beginning about in Earth's twenty-seventh century and going on some two thousand years. Then she began to write about events that go backward in the Hainish history—i.e., events that come closer to the twentieth-century—with the last story occurring in about Earth's twenty-third century.[9]

The Hainish world is based on the story of human expansion, versions of which can be read in myth, history, and fiction. The expulsion of Adam and Eve from the garden, the expansion of the Roman Empire or the Austrian Empire, the settlement of the New World or

THE HAINISH WORLD

the American West are some of the more familiar examples. In science fiction such world-building is called either "galactic empires" or "future history"; Brian Stapleford has noted that this "literary device enables a writer to incarnate virtually any imagined social or biological system, and to bring into contact with it human characters whose worldview is similar to our own."[10] The best known of the writers preceding Le Guin who wrote future histories is Isaac Asimov. He published his Foundation stories in the pulp science fiction magazines and then in the early 1950s reset them into novels and published them as a trilogy.

Of the six Hainish novels the first three can be regarded as the germination of the Hainish history. The distinction between fantasy and science fiction is less clear, especially in *Rocannon's World*, and the relationship between the crises of the individual worlds and the larger Hainish community is not fully explored or developed. Therefore, this chapter will discuss only the three major Hainish novels: *The Left Hand of Darkness*, *The Word for World is Forest*, and *The Dispossessed*. Each of the three novels won the Hugo Award, and *The Left Hand of Darkness* and *The Dispossessed* also won Nebula Awards.

Works prior to *The Left Hand of Darkness* posited some turbulent periods in the formation of a government binding the recontacted worlds together. First called the League of Worlds, either it did not include all the known worlds or the members were not at peace with each other. *Rocannon's World* includes an attack on a League ship by another world and resentment against the League's taxation policy. A later historical period, treated in *City of Illusions,* is known as the Age of the Enemy, a period of war between some of the Hainish worlds and the enemy known as the Shing. The next federation of the worlds is known as the Ekumen, a collective for coordinating contact among the worlds and the exchange of goods and knowledge.

All of the alien encounter stories about the Hainish worlds demonstrate Le Guin's wish for an improved mode for human relations. They grow out of her moral assessment of the contemporary world:

Our curse is alienation, the separation of yang from yin [and the moralization of yang as good, of yin as bad]. Instead of a search for balance and integration, there is a struggle for dominance. Divisions are insisted upon, interdependence is denied. The dualism of value that destroys us, the dualism of superior/inferior, ruler/ ruled, owner/owned, user/used, might give way to what seems to me, from here, a much healthier, sounder, more promising modality of integration and integrity.[11]

The exploration of the "modality of integration and integrity" generates the tension in plot and character, the imagery, and the novels' structure. The integrity of individual people, societies, and worlds can be achieved when the uniqueness and difference of each separate thing is honored. The integration of these diversities is achieved when the interactions and interdependency among them is respected. The search for a mode of human relationships based on integration and integrity is reflected in the structural feature that the three major Hainish novels share: each narrative is told in chapters which shift focus in time period, character, and culture.

In the three major novels Le Guin explores different aspects of developing a modality of integration and integrity. In *The Left Hand of Darkness* she portrays a protagonist who learns how to love the alien. In *The Word for World is Forest* she shows the language difficulties that keep the three central characters from finding a timely solution to intercultural hostilities. In *The Dispossessed* Le Guin uses the protagonist's journey of discovery to explore a social system that seems to achieve integration and integrity.

The Left Hand of Darkness

In *The Left Hand of Darkness* Le Guin worked out what could be called her classic encounter with alienness. It involves the personal encounter that results in increased knowledge of self and other, and it takes place against the background of an international power struggle which threatens the survival of a human community. Caught up in both a personal and an epic struggle, the protagonist, Genly Ai, learns, at great cost, how to love difference. His guide on his journey of discovery is an androgyne, a person who embodies difference.

Le Guin's thought experiment could be stated thus: Let's say that the Ekumen envoy from worlds where humans are either male or female is sent to a planet where the humans are biological androgynes. Furthermore, when the envoy brings the invitation to join the large community of humankind, the two major countries of the planet are approaching war. Retrospectively Le Guin has commented that the themes of the novel are "betrayal and fidelity" and "sex/gender"; she wrote, "I eliminated gender, to find out what was left."[12]

Through Genly Ai, Gethen is offered membership in the Ekumen, a loose federation of eighty-three other Hainish worlds, including Earth, and nearly "three thousand nations."[13] The overall function of the Ekumen is the encouragement and coordination of the exchange of knowledge and goods. As Ai explains to Gethenian diplomats:

The Ekumen as a political entity functions through coordination, not by rule. It does not enforce laws; decisions are reached by council and consent, not by consensus or command. As an economic entity it is immensely active, looking after interworld communication, keeping the balance of trade among the Eighty Worlds (95–96).

THE HAINISH WORLD

The Ekumen is like the twentieth century's attempts to promote worldwide cooperation and peace through such organizations as the League of Nations and the United Nations. It exhibits a condition noted by anthropologists, particularly Alfred Kroeber, where a similar culture emerges among highly developed human societies which are in contact with each other so that the "known world" refers to both culture and land area. Kroeber used the Greek word *oikoumenê* to name this phenomenon of the spread of similar cultural characteristics.[14] The origin of the Ekumen, in terms of its first description in Le Guin's fiction and in terms of its first cause, is found in her short story "Winter's King," which is also set on Gethen. The origin reflects Le Guin's idea of community as process. A young Karhidish king is speaking with the Ekumen ambassador on Gethen:

"The dream of the Ekumen, then, is to restore that truly ancient commonality; to regather all the peoples of all the worlds at one hearth?"

Axt nodded, chewing bread-apple. "To weave some harmony among them, at least. Life loves to know itself, out to its furthest limits; to embrace complexity is its delight. Our difference is our beauty. All these worlds and the various forms and ways of the minds and lives and bodies on them—together they would make a splendid harmony."

"No harmony endures," said the young king.

"None has ever been achieved," said the Plenipo-
tentiary. "The pleasure is in trying."[15]

Genly Ai's diplomatic job is to convince the Gethenians that they will not completely lose their integrity
when they integrate with others. However, a border
dispute between the two major nations of Gethen has
the potential to become a war. Not only is war a condition the Ekumen wishes to prevent, but war would be
especially disastrous on Gethen. The planet is in a permanent Ice Age, and human society has neither the
natural resources nor the time and energy to divert to
war. In both Karhide and Orgoreyn the growing nationalism will increase loyalty to the country and decrease
loyalty to Gethen. The theme of loyalty and betrayal is
acted out against this background of interplanetary,
planetary, and national relationships.

By naming her second concern "gender," Le Guin
is calling attention to those characteristics which are associated with one's sexual identity but which are
learned rather than genetically caused. The Gethenians
have no gender characteristics; they have sexual po-
tency and identity only once a month, during a period
called kemmer. At that time a person becomes sexually
male or female, with no predisposition toward either.
Le Guin discussed the gender experiment in her essay
"Is Gender Necessary? Redux." Her thought experiment, she notes, led her to create a society without war,

THE HAINISH WORLD

exploitation, and "sexuality as a continuous social factor."[16]

The relationship between the two themes of fidelity and gender is shown in the difficulty which the envoy has in completing his mission to bring Gethen into the Ekumen. Unless he can overcome his prejudice against the ambisexual Gethenians and unless he can understand the alienation the Gethenians feel when confronted with the Ekumen, he cannot establish a personal bond of trust and fidelity with them. Without the bond he cannot persuade them as a people to bond with the Ekumen, nor can he dissuade them from war among themselves. Ai's personal difficulties are a microcosm of the complex interplanetary relationships that create the Ekumen.

The extent of Ai's cultural and sexual alienation is evident in the novel's first major dialogue between the two main characters, Ai and Estraven. The conversation, rather than bridging their differences, enhances the solitude felt by each. Ai has preconceptions about how men ought to behave and about how prime ministers ought to discuss affairs of state. Because Estraven does not follow either pattern, Ai concludes that Estraven is dishonest. In this scene, as well as others when Ai distrusts Gethenians, he labels them "womanly." Estraven, on the other hand, raised in a culture where direct verbal confrontation is avoided, also has preconceptions about human behavior. Particularly, he is following the custom of shifgrethor, a duel of language in which each participant circumvents "giving, or accepting, either advice or blame" (139). Estraven fails to see that Ai has not understood his advice.

Ai believes that the importance of his mission and the Ekumen makes the news of Gethenian domestic and international factions irrelevant. He knows well the value of integration of diverse peoples and worlds, but he does not know or understand the value of integrity, the acknowledgment of the uniqueness and difference of each world. Furthermore, his sense of self has become tied to his success on Gethen to the extent that his unguarded thoughts reveal arrogance, impatience, and smugness. Of Estraven he thinks, "Trust him or not, I might still get some use out of him" (11). Such an attitude only increases the alienation he feels by strengthening the barriers he has placed between himself and the Gethenians. When Ai criticizes Estraven, he not only uses characteristics associated with women, he also uses characteristics associated with the shadow. Just as Ged's shadow in *A Wizard of Earthsea* was threatening because it was Ged's own dark, repressed self, so Estraven seems untrustworthy to Ai because Ai has not acknowledged his own female characteristics.

Le Guin presents the novel as Ai's retrospective report for the Ekumen, written in the first person. As the fictive narrator, Ai selects and orders his material. He alternates between the chronological account of his experiences in first person (10 chapters), including

THE HAINISH WORLD

Gethenian myths, passages from Estraven's diary, and an earlier report by an Ekumen observer. He thus recreates for the reader his journey of discovery as an "impatient, inexperienced" (110) young man, and he allows the reader to hear the same Gethenian stories and voices which guided and changed him. He begins his report from the perspective of having completed the journey of discovery, and in that mode he warns the reader about the nature of truth and the multiple voices which will be required for the telling of the story:

I'll make my report as if I told a story, for I was taught as a child on my homeworld that Truth is a matter of the imagination. The soundest fact may fail or prevail in the style of its telling: like that singular organic jewel of our seas, which grows brighter as one woman wears it and, worn by another, dulls and goes to dust. Facts are no more solid, coherent, round, and real than pearls are. But both are sensitive.

The story is not all mine, nor told by me alone. Indeed I am not sure whose story it is; you can judge better. But it is all one, and if at moments the facts seem to alter with an altered voice, why then you can choose the fact you like best; yet none of them are false, and it is all one story (1).

Ai, as fictive narrator, increases the credibility of the story of his transformation by ordering it so that the audience experiences a similar kind of confusion, fragmentation, and alienation caused by both culture and gender shock. Although the opening two paragraphs of the novel speak of shifting truths and voices, they usually do not prepare the first-time reader for the disjunctive experience of reading the first six chapters of the novel.

Although the unity of the novel has been called into question by certain writers, the more persistent criticism of the novel has been that the androgynes are not presented as menwomen. Le Guin is faulted for using the pronoun "he" to refer to them, for portraying them only in those roles usually associated with men (king, statesman, political rebel), and for not portraying them in family and child-rearing roles.[17] Such criticism has been taken seriously by Le Guin, who regards herself as a feminist and regards this novel as her addition to the new women's movement of the 1960s. Her responses, apart from women protagonists in later novels, have included the essay "Is Gender Necessary?", her revision and critique of that essay titled "Is Gender Necessary? Redux," and a reprinting of "Winter's King" with all the pronouns changed to "she." In a recent essay Craig and Diana Barrow have suggested that Le Guin's contribution to feminism is that she "posits typically biased heterosexual males as her main audience" and has created a protagonist with whom they can identify and so have their awareness about gender identity sharpened. The authors perceptively point out, however, that her female audience looks to "vicariously appreciate Estraven as 'manwoman' rather than man" and may be disappointed when he is not depicted in unique roles.[18]

As a character involved in both themes of the novel, however, Genly Ai's increasingly androgynous behavior is part of his response to both the culture and gender shock from which he suffers. As his experiences enable him to break through the barriers he has erected between himself and the Gethenians, he becomes more patient, accepting, capable of reciprocating love, less rationalist, less dependent on the certainty of his beliefs.

In his chronological narrative Ai shows that both the experience of the Foretelling and the imprisonment in Orgoreyn force him to the margins of "normal" experience, and both times he recognizes the uniqueness of the Gethenians and the sameness, their humanness. In the Foretelling he sees the female side of Faxe as heroic and creative, and he recognizes the Gethenians' superiority in the use of paraverbal powers.[19] At the Pulefen Prison Farm, betrayed and silenced, his own mission now clearly thwarted, Ai is horrified to find that the Orgota prisoners are equally stifled; they are given drugs that eliminate the kemmer cycle.

More subtly, Ai has also been reporting on another way his transformation occurred; he has been including Gethenian myths from "very long ago" in his chronological account. Their significance was announced in the opening two paragraphs of the story when Ai asserted that everything in his report was "true"—in other words, that what he experienced in hearing the myths was as valid as what he experienced in interacting with the leaders of Karhide and Orgoreyn. The myths not only help explain specific features of the Gethenian culture, they also help explain the philosophy which has been the foundation of that culture.

The Gethenian tales augment Ai's experiences and guide him toward a more complete understanding of the Gethenian people and of the relevance of their uniqueness to himself. The tales, then, ease Ai toward the lowering of his own barriers against seeing the Gethenians as individuals and particularly accepting Estraven as a person. Ai has placed the tales so that the specific action of each precedes his account of a related experience. For example, "The Nineteenth Day," a parable about the dangers of trying to use foretelling to eliminate the uncertainty of life, is immediately followed by the chapter detailing Ai's visit to the foretellers at Otherhord. But each tale also continues to augment the meaning of Ai's experiences throughout the novel. Ai has selected tales which use incidents and personal names similar to his actual experiences. This similarity, N. B. Hayles has noted, "creates a feeling of déjà vu and allows Le Guin to suggest connections without making them explicit."[20] For example, "The Place Inside the Blizzard" is related to the next chapter, in which Estraven's exile from Karhide is announced. But the truth of the myth is borne out in Estraven's past and subsequent actions. The myth's account of the incest violation and suicide seems echoed in Estraven's past relationship with his brother Arek and Arek's death. Further, like Getheren in the myth, Estraven's actions continue to affect his home country.

The tales suggest that in addition to the linear pattern there is another way of thinking about and recording one's experiences—a circular or spiral pattern, a movement backward in time which discloses a truth which is relevant to present time. The reader of Ai's report must work backward and forward among the chapters to understand the "one story" Ai is telling. *The Left Hand of Darkness* challenges the reader, in the same way that Ai's Gethenian experience challenged him, to see things from the perspective of diversity rather than of opposing dualities.

The five myths that Ai has selected all deal with the problem of dualities and the individuals' acceptance or refusal of that which is different. Acceptance leads to acts which are creative; denial leads to acts which are destructive.

Frequently in Western thought dualities are viewed as opposites, competing for dominance. In the Eastern tradition, particularly in Taoism, with which Le Guin is familiar, dualities are viewed as correlates or complements. So engrained is the concept of duality as opposition that it is difficult to find English words for the Taoist concept of duality as complements. Genly Ai, in summarizing his perception of Estraven, uses the phrase "both and one" (187), and he refers to the physical image of the yang-yin circle. Le Guin turns to metaphor for assistance, using the web, network, or woven fabric as a way of depicting the interdependence and independence of all things: male and female, fidelity and betrayal, myth and reality, light and dark, linear and circular, fact and imagination. Acceptance of dualities as complementaries means, then, that there is some truth in each, but there is no complete truth in only one.

With the help of the myths Ai comes to understand that meaningful vows, those that change the life of an individual, a nation, or an intergalactic federation, begin with the pledges of individuals; conversely they end with betrayals by individuals. In the myths the vow of fidelity which symbolizes all vows of personal trust and fidelity is the vow of kemmering, the pledge of fidelity between self and other, I and Thou. The most complex of the tales and the one that reverberates throughout Ai's report is "Estraven the Traitor." Placed in the middle of the novel, it echoes the difficult political relationships between Karhide and Orgoreyn, as well as between Gethen and the Ekumen; the painful relationship between Estraven and his lost brother; and the significance of the personal vow for future peace.

The Foretelling, Pulefen Prison Farm, and the myths help Ai recognize that his mission is a dual one of integrity and integration. The final breakdown of barriers occurs during the journey across the ice. Although there are many factors in that journey which further prepare Ai for the ultimate self change, it is finally the sexual tension between them that enables Ai to commit himself to Estraven. Unable to ignore Estraven's double sexuality, and prepared by his previous experiences and knowledge of the Gethenians, Ai finds that all of his resistance collapses:

> And I saw then again, and for good, what I had always been afraid to see, and had pretended not to see in him: that he was a woman as well as a man. Any need to explain the sources of that fear vanished with the fear; what I was left with was, at last, acceptance of him as he was (173).

Each sees clearly the different sexual nature of the other, and out of that tension is created a new relationship. It exemplifies that specific and abstract relationship Estraven identifies when he recites "Tormer's Lay":

> *Light is the left hand of darkness*
> *and darkness the right hand of light.*
> *Two are one, life and death, lying*
> *together like lovers in kemmer,*
> *like hands joined together,*
> *like the end and the way* (164).

It is a relationship based on human characteristics, not gender roles. It recognizes the equality of both people and depends on the cooperation and nurturing of both people. It gives joy and makes each vulnerable to pain caused by the other. It consists of sharing many intimacies but not that of sex. Estraven gives Ai all the knowledge and care he can to survive on the ice; Ai gives Estraven the ability to mindspeak, which increases their intimacy but is also a source of pain. That Estraven hears Ai's voice as his brother Arek's reminds them of their closeness in a brotherlike love *and* of their distance, for Ai is not Arek.

Genly Ai is changed by this love, although what his future dealings with monosexed people and double-sexed people will be is unclear at the end of the novel. Ai has become more like the patient Gethenians. After sending the call to his ship, he muses, "I did not know if I had done right to send it. I had come to accept such uncertainties with a quiet heart" (196). He has also accepted the ambivalence of truth. After telling King Argaven that Estraven and he served the same "master"— "Mankind,"—he thinks:

As I spoke I did not know if what I said was true. True in part; an aspect of the truth. It would be no less true to say that Estraven's acts had risen out of pure personal loyalty, a sense of responsibility and friendship towards one single human being, myself. Nor would that be the whole truth (204–05).

Circling back through the novel from this point, the reader realizes that all through the report Ai has pointed

THE HAINISH WORLD

out the partial truth of his assertions. N. B. Hayles notes, "No truth is allowed to stand as the entire truth; every insight is presented as partial, subject to revision and another perspective."[21] The most prominent dualities of male and female, betrayal and fidelity, are seen to be conditions that change like the pearls Ai spoke of in the opening paragraphs of his report. To Argaven, Estraven betrayed him when he sought to end the dispute between Karhide and Orgoreyn by moving the farmers out of the disputed boundary area. Estraven believes he was being loyal to all Karhiders by saving lives and avoiding war. Fidelity to a larger group of humanity or to a different set of principles is viewed as betrayal by the original group, and there is some truth in each judgment. Even between Estraven and Ai are partial truths about betrayal and fidelity. Ai dreams that Estraven betrayed Ai by dying: "he had gone on by himself, deserting us, deserting me" (200). And when Ai must call down his ship and proceed with Gethen's joining the Ekumen even though he had promised Estraven he would clear his name first, Ai sees the truth in naming his own actions as betrayal. The concepts of betrayal and fidelity are, finally, complementary; out of the tension of the truth of each, Ai has a larger perspective which will forever affect his relationships with the other and the vow of fidelity which must be at the heart of those relationships; at the conclusion of his mission on Gethen he has truly become a representative of the Ekumen.

UNDERSTANDING URSULA K. LE GUIN

Perhaps the Ekumen recognized that this process of transformation usually occurs in the First Mobile's mission, for he is not given the official role of ambassador until after the agreement has been made. As Genly Ai tells Estraven:

Alone, I cannot change your world. But I can be changed by it. Alone, I must listen, as well as speak. Alone, the relationship I finally make, if I make one, is not impersonal and not only political: it is individual, it is personal, it is both more and less than political. Not We and They; not I and It; but I and Thou. Not political, not pragmatic, but mystical (181).

The creative tension that arises from recognizing the complementarity of dualities and leads to a new wholeness is caught by Le Guin in the opening image of the novel—the king using blood mortar to affix the keystone and thereby create the arch. Remembering this act, Ai uses it metaphorically when he returns to Karhide: "My friend being dead, I must accomplish the thing he died for. I must set the keystone in the arch" (202). The blood mortar in the arch symbolizes Estraven's death and reminds the reader of the risk which is always involved with the vow of fidelity—the risk of pain and loss. In Estraven's death Gethen has lost a person of vision; in joining the Ekumen the people have lost the perception of themselves as the "proper" human form. Genly Ai has lost a guide and friend, and in loving the androgyne has lost the perception of his race as the "proper" human form. The arch itself, the new creation, symbolizes the love between Estraven and Ai which helps create the bond between Gethen and the Ekumen. Out of love for that which is different, new relationships and perceptions are brought into existence.

The Word for World is Forest

The bridging of differences in *The Left Hand of Darkness* is achieved as Genly Ai and Estraven communicate their contrasting perceptions of gender and sex, loyalty and betrayal, self and other. In *The Word for World is Forest* Le Guin depicts a dark chapter in the Hainish history when contact with the alien leads to war rather than to an alliance. The contact between soldiers and loggers from Earth and the natives of the heavily forested planet Athshe fails because neither group finds a language for connection and exchange. The novel explores how each group's language both reflects and shapes its perception of reality; no shared language is found to construct a reality in which the Terrans and Athsheans achieve integration and integrity. The shared language that is needed is not just a matter of grammar and vocabulary, but also of altered attitudes toward self, community, and world for which mutually understood names can be found. Where naming was examined in Le Guin's fantasy as a metaphysical issue, a search for a thing's essence, here in the science fiction naming is examined in the context of social and political systems.

The novel's title announces its focus on language. The relationship between the Athsheans and their external world is revealed in the fact that "the Athshean word for *world* is also the word for *forest*";[22] further, the relationship between the Athsheans and their internal world is revealed in the fact that the "word 'dream' . . . was also the word for 'root'" (100). On the planet Athshe the natives have developed a culture that is an integral part of the forest which covers the planet. They are similar to the Gethenians in developing within their planet's ecology. Nowhere has land been cleared to provide room for the human species or to provide resources for extensive technological development. Instead they are a decentralized society, living in scattered villages that fit into the tree roots and soil. Integration has also been achieved internally; they have learned to control their dreams so that their actions result from both the subconscious in dreaming and from the conscious mind in the nondreaming state. They speak of the equality of "dream-time" and "world-time."

Contrasted to the nonaggressive, ecologically sensitive culture are the representatives from Earth's culture. Having nearly destroyed their own planet by pollution and by exhaustion of natural resources, they have now come to exploit Athshe's forests. Le Guin's thought experiment could be reconstructed as follows: Let's say that the planet of a pacifist culture is colonized by a logging crew under the control of the military from Earth, and let's say further that the natives recognize the Terrans as humans, but the Terrans do not recognize that the little green, furry natives are human.

Le Guin has expressed her dissatisfaction with the strident tone of the novella. Although she published it in 1972, she had written it while spending the year 1968–69 in England. In a 1977 introduction to the novel she explained the circumstances that led her to say, "I never wrote a story more easily, fluently, surely—and with less pleasure." Bitterly troubled by the Vietnam war, and without the outlet of the peace movement in which she had been participating in the United States, she wrote this story, first titled *The Little Green Men*, and was unable to keep it from becoming "a preachment."[23] Certainly in contrasting the two cultures, as Gary K. Wolfe has pointed out, she sometimes exaggerates the characteristics of their representatives.[24]

What may have led many readers and reviewers to dismiss this novel as propagandistic is that the voices of three characters dominate the novel: Captain Davidson, leader of one of the Terran logging camps; Selver, a native of Athshe; and Lyubov, the ethnographer from India. There is no relief from the triangle, and their actions seem exaggerated because many of the dramatic events happen outside the narrative.

This characteristic is, in fact, one of the novel's strengths. Le Guin has written an antiwar novel which keeps almost all the actual planning, strategy, and execution of battle action off the page. What the novel does feature are the mental states of the three principal characters; Le Guin goes behind the events of war and murder into the minds where the decisions are made to commit or stop such acts. The drama of the novel comes from the tension of the differences among the three principals and from the tension within each individual. The differences among them are emphasized when Le Guin alternates the focal character and point of view from chapter to chapter; Davidson's three chapters are 1, 4, 7; Lyubov's are 3 and 5; Selver's are 2, 6, 8. The alternation also mirrors the isolation of each character.

The use of the limited omniscient point of view for Davidson's and Lyubov's chapters makes them read like interior monologues. Thus the reader experiences Davidson as the army captain who is relentlessly and enjoyably planning how to conquer the inferior people and hostile elements of nature. The reader experiences Lyubov as a scientist trying to do his job well and yet abide by his personal and professional ethics. The use of omniscient point of view for Selver's chapters allows Le Guin to portray the Athshean culture with some detail and yet still keep it alien. She portrays several Athsheans besides Selver and does not write extensive passages for Selver that read like interior monologues.

THE HAINISH WORLD

Captain Don Davidson's monologues expose the reader to a mind that hates what is different, beginning with the Athsheans but extending finally to even the men under his command. Le Guin bombards the reader with his hostilities and prejudices in sentence fragments. She also distinguishes the Davidson chapters by his vocabulary, particularly animal metaphors and words with unpleasant connotations which create a snarling, sneering tone for many passages. Davidson reveals himself and, in the ethic of the novel, condemns himself by the language he uses.

Names are value-ladened categories that Davidson uses to identify the adversarial relationship between himself and the person or idea or event which confronts him. His nouns, adjectives, and metaphors leave no room for ambivalence; he essentially sees the world from an "us versus them" perspective. His most prominent language habit that reveals more about himself than it does about the thing spoken of is using derogatory animal metaphors for people. Men who obey the colonel are "sheep"; the Hainish representative from the League is a "little grey ape" (76); the women who have just joined the colony are "prime human stock" (1); the Athsheans are like fish or ants or beetles. He also uses the colony's common nickname, creechies, for the Athsheans. A derivative of "creatures," the name avoids assigning them human status. When he calls them "green monkeys," one could argue that he is not being metaphorical; to Davidson the Athsheans are green and they are monkeys; he does not believe they are humans which the Hainish brought to this planet.

Davidson's language is also distinguished by his use of connotative labels for himself and for others. People of whom he disapproves are dismissed as "alien-lover," "traitor," "effeminate," "old woman," "soybean-sucker." The connotative labels he proudly uses for himself are "conquistador," "savior," and "world-tamer," revealing his need to be superior and powerful. "Conquistador" is a double-sided word, depending on one's perspective. It recalls either the heroic explorer or the villainous exploiter of new worlds.

Davidson's mental rigidity is both a cause and an effect of his insanity. In order to maintain the categories he has set up barriers which allow him to dismiss or refute contrary evidence. One effective barrier is simply to label anyone who proposes other ideas as having "gone spla," gone insane; by attacking the person rather than the idea he never has to consider the idea. A second effective barrier is his fixed belief that humans, a word synonymous with people from Earth, are the center of life in the universe. This belief justifies any exploitation of another culture or environment. A third barrier is his belief that the way things are is the way they should be, or more accurately stated, the way he perceives things to be is the way they should be. This refrain, expressed as "It just happened to be the way

THE HAINISH WORLD

things are" (154), frees him from having to verbally defend complex ideas. For example, it justifies his racism:

Some men, especially the asiatiforms and hindi types, are actually born traitors. Not all, but some. Certain other men are born saviors. It just happened to be the way they were made, like being of euraf descent, or like having a good physique; it wasn't anything he claimed credit for (78–79).

In contrast to the other two major characters, Davidson is not self-aware. In sharp contrast to Lyubov, who has difficulty acting because he is so acutely aware of how he reacts to things, Davidson is unable to reflect on the various influences that led him to hold a particular belief or make a particular decision. In sharp contrast to Selver, Davidson is not in touch with his subconscious. Dreams, a mental function where the subconscious is made manifest, are dismissed by Davidson as being unreal and a waste of time. The whole forest of Athshe, which can be interpreted as a metaphor for the subconscious,[25] frightens Davidson. The only relationship he knows is mastery; as he says, "The only time a man is really and entirely a man is when he's just had a woman or just killed another man" (81). Both Lyubov and Selver recognize the self-hatred and fear that lie at the center of Davidson's actions. Lyubov comments,

"It's himself whom the murderer kills; only he has to do it over, and over, and over" (103).

For Lyubov's two chapters Le Guin uses a different style to portray the mental state of the anthropologist who observes, studies his data, and tries to understand the Athsheans. Not only does Lyubov use technical terms, he also deals with new situations in a scientific way. Chapter 5, for example, gives Lyubov's thoughts as he tries to puzzle out answers to questions about Athshean behavior. He proposes answers, then criticizes them, raises more questions, and is reluctant to fix on a single answer. His intelligence and interest in language are evident in literary allusions, wordplay, and references to his own writing.

In contrast to Davidson he is self-reflexive and analytical. For example, when confronted with the news that the League of Worlds has been formed, Lyubov, unlike Davidson, accepts the information, but only after analyzing his own initial reaction:

They were in league, and lying. This thought went through Lyubov's mind; he considered it, decided it was a reasonable but unwarranted suspicion, a defense-mechanism, and discarded it. Some of the military staff, however, trained to compartmentalize their thinking, specialists in self-defense, would accept it as unhesitatingly as he discarded it. They must believe that anyone claiming a sudden new authority was a liar or conspirator (66–67).

THE HAINISH WORLD

Lyubov's self-reflexiveness keeps him from becoming as insane as Davidson, but his head suffers in another way; he has migraine headaches. Lyubov is caught in the position of being a colonial representative and yet realizing that colonial practices are threatening the existence of the culture he is studying. He is a civilian specialist with neither respect nor authority. The more he treats the Athsheans as humans, the more he is rejected by the colonials. Yet Lyubov is the only individual who has the knowledge to serve as a bridge, to bring creative action out of the contact between the two alien societies.

Le Guin shows that Lyubov's breakthroughs in understanding the Athshean culture and in understanding Selver occur when he learns the meaning of certain Athshean words. It is Lyubov who explains that in the Athshean culture the word for world is *forest*. When he describes the Athsheans he chooses a forest metaphor: "They're a static, stable, uniform society. They have no history. Perfectly integrated, and wholly unprogressive. You might say that like the forest they live in, they've attained a climax state" (61–62). Lyubov's initial discomfort in the forest, the "mass and jumble of various competitive lives, . . . the total vegetable indifference to the presence of mind" (88), makes him appreciate the Athshean humility, the acknowledgment that they are only one of many forms of life on this planet.

As Lyubov learns about Athshean psychology, however, he comes to appreciate the confidence which emerges from their belief that "Athshean man was branch and root" (89). Root, that which stabilizes and nourishes the tree, is akin to dreaming, which stabilizes the Athsheans. That the Athshean word for root is also the word for dream suggests metaphorically that the roots of the forest symbolize the unconscious and the forest symbolizes the integration of the subconscious and the diversity of consciousness. Lyubov realizes that his headaches indicate he has not achieved this integration, the ability to "balance your sanity not on the razor's edge of reason but on the double support, the fine balance, of reason and dream" (99).

In Lyubov's second chapter Le Guin conflates two texts: the Athshean pronouncement that Selver is a god and Lyubov's final report on the Athsheans to his superiors. Using the dictionary he and Selver made, Lyubov discovers that the Athshean word for god *(sha-ab)* means translator, "one who could speak aloud the perceptions of the subconscious" (106). This linking of the two "realities, . . . the dream-time and the world-time" (106) is, Lyubov realizes, "to act. To do a new thing. To change or to be changed, radically, from the root. For the root is the dream" (106). To be able to put into words the experience of the subconscious is to create a new reality. But even with this new knowledge Lyubov is unable to answer the question of how the Athsheans changed in order to be able to murder. His final attempt to answer what is unanswerable expresses again the idea that language is the key act in world creation;

thinking of Selver he wonders, "Was he speaking his own language, or was he speaking Captain Davidson's?" (107).

Following these thoughts Lyubov writes his own text in which he creates a fictional world—a report which depicts the Athshean village "going about its business as usual" (109). Centralville was thus totally unprepared for the brutal Athshean attack two nights later. Could he have done more? Could he have prevented the attack by working with one side or the other? Like Davidson, did his compartmentalized thinking prevent him from seeing that he too could be a "god," a link between two cultures? Or is he, in fact, a god by letting his subconscious dictate the kind of report he wrote and thereby saving the Athsheans? The significance of Lyubov's crisis is that it raises such questions, not that it leads to a right answer.

Because the Selver chapters are told from the omniscient point of view, the reader never experiences the immersion in his mind that is experienced in the Davidson and Lyubov chapters. Selver remains alien, known of but not fully understood. Le Guin devotes three chapters to him, but not all the information comes from his perspective alone; the thoughts of other Athsheans are included, as well as conversations of which Selver is not a part. The style of the chapters, however, is distinctly different from that of Davidson's and Lyubov's chapters and reveals yet another perception of the world reflected in language. The language which

UNDERSTANDING URSULA K. LE GUIN

distinguishes Selver's chapters consists of images and metaphors that reflect the Athshean integration with their environment. Further, there is no inequality suggested in the language used to describe events from world-time and events from dream-time. The dominant images and metaphors of the Athsheans are of forest and path, but metaphors of animals are also important.

The Selver chapters reproduce what it would be like to be part of a race which saw itself as one of several living forms collaborating to produce the world. Le Guin thrusts the reader into the insider's view in the lyrical opening paragraph of chapter 2:

No way was clear, no light unbroken, in the forest. Into wind, water, sunlight, starlight, there always entered leaf and branch, bole and root, the shadowy, the complex. Little paths ran under the branches, around the boles, over the roots; they did not go straight, but yielded to every obstacle, devious as nerves. . . . The colors of rust and sunset kept changing in the hanging leaves of the copper willows, and you could not say even whether the leaves of the willows were brownish-red, or reddish-green, or green (25–26).

The description places the forest in the foreground and the other features of nature in the background; the paths make way for the forest. Ideas of color, age, voices, kinship are all expressed in forest metaphors. The Athsheans' decentralized sociopolitical structure is modeled after their forest world. The clans and villages remain as separate and distinct as different species of trees, and yet their overall similarity is as evident as a forest. People are identified by clans, which are named after trees, and clans form villages.

Especially significant for giving the insider's view, however, is Le Guin's use of metaphors of forest and path to express mental states and sociopolitical conditions. To the Athsheans mental health is a condition of being in touch with one's roots. As Selver recovers from leading the first attack on Smith Camp, he gradually resumes the complex, daily cycle of dreaming; his relief is expressed in terms of forest conditions: "He had feared that he was cut off from his roots, that he had gone too far into the dead land of action ever to find his way back to the springs of reality. Now, though the water was very bitter, he drank again" (38). When Selver tries to explain to other Athsheans what the Terrans are like—the people who are destroying the forest and who rape, castrate, and kill the Athsheans—he suggests that "they have left their roots behind them" (44).

The path metaphor is used by the Athsheans to express tradition and change as well as mental health. The Old Dreamer, Coro Mena, in trying to assess whether or not Selver is insane, asks, "Can you walk the road your dream goes?" (32), meaning, Can you follow the route of the subconscious and so learn what it has to say about your fears? Just as new paths have to be found through the forest as the trees and undergrowth change, so the Athsheans must be able to adjust. As a god Selver comes "through the forest, . . . where leaves fall, where trees fall" (35), meaning that he is not following a path that already exists. Because Selver teaches them how to kill and destroy, he is called the "son of forest-fire" (46).

Where Davidson simply used animal metaphors to signal someone of little or no value, the Athsheans criticize the yumens by comparing them only to animals that are dangerous or are pests—snakes, stinging ants, insects that feed on carrion. In fact, when Selver feels the animal metaphor is being used as a synonym for the humans, he hastens to correct the speaker. The headwoman of Berre says the yumens are "great naked spiders," and Selver asserts, "They are men, men, like us, men." And she adds, "Oh, my dear lord god, I know it, I only meant they *look* like spiders" (137).

Where Davidson's language created a world of adversarial relationships, the Athshean language shows relationships of continuities, of dualities that are not competitions. Just as Estraven and Ai recognize the necessity of shadows to find their way across the snow, so the Athsheans recognize the shadow as an integral part of the forest and of their mental health, where it symbolizes the subconscious, the repressed, the nonrational which their complex form of controlled dreaming allows them to deal with. To the Athsheans world-time and dream-time are a collaborative duality.[26] Both are realities, and they are of equal significance; a speaker slips from one to the other, accepting the validity of each.

Their collaboration in a single experience is also creative. It can show the dreamer what action is appropriate. For example, the event that makes more certain Selver's return to sanity is his experience with Lyubov on the night of Lyubov's death. It is difficult to ascertain whether there is a world-time conversation between them or whether Lyubov is already dead and the conversation occurs in dream-time. Lyubov first asks Selver which one of them is the prisoner, and Selver replies, "Neither, both, how do I know?" (117). Superficially it is a dialogue about who won the battle; more deeply it is a dialogue about whose ethic, whose world perspective, whose definition of "man," is in control. Has Selver become so much like the "yumens" that he is putting up barriers in his mind as Davidson did to allow him to justify war and murder? Then Selver asks Lyubov, "Why aren't you like the others?" to which Lyubov insists, "I am like them. A man. Like them. Like you" (117). This message that "we are alike" is what allows Selver to complete his tasks as a god and then return to more normal Athshean paths.

The tension within Selver's chapters rises from the same increasing insanity that characterizes Davidson and Lyubov. Selver's actions reveal the mental state of one who has changed and who continues to choose to go against his culture's ethic in order to ensure the culture's survival. As Coro Mena says to him, "You've done what you had to do, and it was not right" (33–34). Of the three principals, Selver is the only one who returns to some kind of mental health; Davidson falls deeper into madness, and Lyubov dies. Selver's scarred face remains as a symbol of the irremediable physical and mental damage done by the Terrans.

Selver's concluding actions as a god are to ensure the end of the killing. He negotiates a treaty between the Athsheans and Terrans, and he gives Davidson the gift of "not killing" (160). Rather than turning Davidson over to the Terrans who would surely execute him, Selver treats him like one of his own people who has gone insane and is dangerous; he sends him to complete his life on an isolated island.

The policy of isolating the murderer has its obverse in the conclusion of the novel—isolation of the potential victim. Lyubov's work is instrumental in bringing about the League ban on Athshe—the removal of all Terrans and the promise that no League members will return for several generations and then only to study. Lyubov's question as to who is the prisoner makes clear the bleak ending of the novel; in order to ensure their survival the League has isolated the Athsheans. But, as Selver tells the Hainishman, he and his people have been forever changed by learning to murder their own species, and Selver carries around with him in his subconscious both Lyubov and Davidson. The Athsheans have learned of life on other worlds; like the Gethenians they can no longer regard themselves as a society entire unto them-

THE HAINISH WORLD

selves. In light of Le Guin's presentation in *The Left Hand of Darkness* of the value of joining the larger human community, the League's decision to set Athshe beyond the League boundaries must surely be judged in the same words Coro Mena used for Selver: "You've done what you had to do, and it was not right."

The Dispossessed

Although Le Guin specifically mentions the Vietnam war as a source of her anger and frustration that led to the writing of *The Word for World is Forest*, that event is only one of several in her contemporary 1960s and 1970s world that could make her lose hope that humankind would ever find the language, ethics, and technology to lessen alienation and find the "modality of integration and integrity" that she searches for in her Hainish world. Retrospectively, one could say that Le Guin prepared herself to write a Hainish novel about an individual who achieves integrity and integration in his personal, professional, and social life. Between the writing of *The Word for World is Forest* in 1968–69 and the publication of *The Dispossessed* in 1974, Le Guin wrote other works about worlds gone awry (*The Lathe of Heaven*, 1971, and *The Tombs of Atuan*, 1970–71); used settings closer to her contemporary society (*The Lathe of Heaven* is set in Portland in the twenty-first century;

"Vaster than Empires and More Slow," a Hainish short story, is set just after the League was formed); and explored the limits and costs of utopia ("Vaster than Empires," 1971, and "The Ones Who Walk Away from Omelas," 1973). In the midst of these explorations, however, she wrote *The Farthest Shore* (1972), which brought the Earthsea series to a close and recounted Ged and Arren's successful search for the cause of the loss of faith in magic and the restoration of the king to Earthsea.

Having explored dystopias and questioned the limits of utopias, Le Guin discovered in her imagination a character who stated he was "a citizen of Utopia" and who became the protagonist of *The Dispossessed: An Ambiguous Utopia*, the novel that closes the Hainish series. In her essay "Science Fiction and Mrs. Brown," Le Guin describes the process of discovering Shevek. He was a physicist, in appearance like Robert Oppenheimer, with a "personality, which was most attractive . . . , I mean, as a flame to a moth." She records that "in the process of trying to find out who and what Shevek was, I found out a great deal else, and thought as hard as I was capable of thinking, about society, about my world, and about myself."[27]

The Dispossessed has as its thought experiment: Let's see what would happen if a theoretical physicist came to maturity in a century-old anarchist society just when it is falling toward a structured government. Let's say further that he needs the stimulation of physicists on other worlds to continue his work, but no travel between worlds has been allowed by his society. Le Guin compounds her experiment, as indicated by the novel's subtitle, "An Ambiguous Utopia," by questioning whether such a society is a utopia.

"Utopia," a word first used by Sir Thomas More as the name of his imaginary ideal society in *Utopia* (1516), is a play on two Greek phrases: *"ou topos:* no place, and *eu topos:* good place."[28] Its etymology raises the issue of ambiguity: Is it a fantastic place of the imagination, or is it a model for human society? Le Guin labels her utopia "ambiguous" in order to call into question what she perceives as the traditional characteristics of utopia in Western literature. In a 1980 essay she asserted, "Utopia has been yang. In one way or another, from Plato on, utopia has been the big yang motorcycle trip. Bright, dry, clear, strong, firm, active, aggressive, lineal, progressive, creative, expanding, advancing, and hot." It is totalitarian and depends on reason "as the controlling power." Rejecting that model, Le Guin offers the "yin utopia": "it would be dark, wet, obscure, weak, yielding, passive, participatory, circular, cyclical, peaceful, nurturant, retreating, contracting, and cold."[29]

To develop her nontraditional utopia Le Guin does not use the techniques usually found in utopian novels. Her protagonist, instead of being a traveler to utopia, is a citizen of utopia. Instead of little significant conflict and long expository passages (usually between the traveler and a utopian or a citizen of the traveler's home), Le Guin shows a utopian society in danger.

Anarres is a world of scarcity. Mostly desert, the planet provides little that enables the people to enjoy luxuries or to build up their reserves. A four-year drought leads to famine during which a mother kills her baby because she has no food for it, a train engineer kills people on the tracks who are mobbing a food train, and food rations are reduced for those who are ill. Anarres is nontraditional in another way; no person or group is overseeing the society so as to ensure happiness for all because the society is based on philosophical anarchism.

In 1975, having written a short story about Odo, the founder of Anarres ("The Day Before the Revolution"), Le Guin explained her attraction to the philosophy of anarchism:

Odonianism is anarchism. Not the bomb-in-the-pocket stuff, which is terrorism . . . ; not the social-Darwinist "libertarianism" of the far right; but anarchism, as prefigured in early Taoist thought, and expounded by Shelley and Kropotkin, Goldman and Goodman. Anarchism's principal target is the authoritarian State (capitalist or socialist); its principal moral-practical theme is cooperation (solidarity, mutual aid). It is the most idealistic, and to me the most interesting, of all political theories.[30]

THE HAINISH WORLD

"Anarchy" connotes disorder, lawlessness, and violent overthrow of the government. However, the word also denotes a philosophy based on a belief that moral responsibility rests solely with the individual and on a model of evolution that views cooperation, not competition, as the key to survival.

Describing Le Guin's utopianism or philosophical anarchism might cause a reader to expect a novel that is a political handbook, reminiscent of Robert Heinlein's *The Moon Is a Harsh Mistress* (1966), which details how a colonial moon (with the aid of a supercomputer) might successfully win a war for independence with its parent world. Certainly the political system is a primary interest, but the focus of the novel is on the protagonist Shevek—temporal physicist, social reformer, son, partner, father. And necessarily so, for with no government to do the business of the society, the individuals are the society. "We don't leave Anarres, because we *are* Anarres," Shevek argues with his young friends.[31] So connected are the protagonist Shevek and the utopian anarchy of his homeworld that a reader must say of them, as Ai says of Estraven in *The Left Hand of Darkness*, "both and one."

Both and one describes many aspects of this novel. A reader is challenged to experience integrity and integration in the novel's images, structure, scientific novum, and social relationships. The novel opens with the image of a wall, which invites the reader to approach the work with a both-and, not an either-or, perspective. "There was a wall. It did not look important. . . . But the idea was real. . . . Like all walls it was ambiguous, two-faced. What was inside it and what was outside it depended upon which side of it you were on" (1). Wishing to prevent Urrasti people and influence from entering their society, the Anarresti built a wall around the spaceport so that the only contact between the two societies would be the exchange of goods. In consensus reality the image recalls the incarceration of Japanese-Americans during World War II, the Iron Curtain, and the Berlin Wall. As a recurring image in the novel it suggests the ambiguity of both physical and psychological walls, dividing national and international communities, being both enabling and imprisoning.

A second image in the opening chapter which suggests the richness of the both-and perspective is that of the two worlds, Anarres and Urras, circling each other. They can be regarded as having a hierarchical relationship, that is, planet and moon, parent and colony; but the novel questions who is parenting whom. They can also be regarded as having an egalitarian relationship. In the background of the novel are the other eight known Hainish worlds, who have recognized the need for an intergalactic organization. Figuratively they have the opportunity to circle one another in a relationship of integrity and integration.

These ambiguous images of walls and circling worlds help prepare the reader for the novel's structure

THE HAINISH WORLD

and meaning. Rather than narrating Shevek's experiences chronologically, Le Guin alternates between Shevek's first thirty-eight years on Anarres and his single year on Urras. The different periods in Shevek's life thus circle each other in the reader's mind, separate yet integrated, exchanging roles of cause and effect. Further, the images help prepare the reader for understanding Shevek's search for a general temporal theory that will combine the concepts of time as sequency and as simultaneity.

If the novel is read in the order in which it is printed (chapters 1 through 13), the reader experiences Shevek's life both sequentially and cyclically. To discuss the novel in this order, however, would result in considerable repetition, since the effects of juxtaposing chapters are often similar; to discuss Shevek's life chronologically is also unsatisfactory because it deletes the very complexity that Le Guin has created. Therefore, in an effort to reflect the novel's complexity and yet be economical, this discussion will follow the overall rising and falling action of the novel. The early stages of each part of Shevek's life will be examined in terms of his increasing knowledge about his personal, professional, and social commitments (chapters 2–8 and 1–7); followed by the climax of each (chapters 9 and 10), and the resolution (chapters 11–13).

Shevek's efforts to understand his personal and social function in society and to find the equations for the general temporal theory are depicted as the familiar cir-

cular journey of discovery which Le Guin used in the
Earthsea novels and the previous Hainish novels; the
journey outward eventually involves a return to one's
roots before moving outward again.

Shevek's first journey, which explains why Shevek
made the second journey, begins in chapter 2. Through
seven episodes from his first twenty years, Le Guin
shows Shevek encountering the imperfections of this
utopian anarchy and yet sharpening his personal
commitment to it. In fairly dramatic ways Shevek
experiences the conflict that lies at the heart of every
adolescent's journey to adulthood and citizenship—the
desire for personal independence in conflict with the
need to sacrifice personal liberty for the sake of the continuance of a human community. The conflict is especially significant in an anarchist society, for without
government it is the individual's commitment which ensures the community's existence.

The early Anarres chapters (4, 6, 8) depict Shevek
learning the meaning of the promise, that act which is
central to Anarres's origin and continued existence.
Shevek moves from feeling isolated from his society to
committing himself to a female partner and then to social reform.

The promise that binds Anarres together is the vow
of fidelity to each other to do that which ensures the
continuation of a society without government, dominance, and ownership; it is a vow of human solidarity,
a moral commitment to mutual aid and cooperation.

THE HAINISH WORLD

Shevek's journey into adulthood begins when he faces the broken promise in his own life. Sabul and Shevek violate the promise when they bargain over the publication of Shevek's work. His renewed contact with his mother, Rulag, reminds Shevek of the broken promise between his mother and father. Shevek refuses Rulag's offer of further association, but as she leaves, he begins to cry: "He gave way to the fear that had come with her, the sense of the breaking of promises, the incoherence of time" (110).

In response to the violated promise Shevek seeks to balance his commitment to his fellow beings with his need for freedom to develop his talent in physics. But "his efforts to break out of his essential isolation were, in fact, a failure; . . . the work came first, but it went nowhere" (140). Bedap names the cause of Shevek's suffering, "the wall," which Bedap identifies as the power structure that is beginning to appear everywhere on Anarres: "public opinion, . . . the unadmitted, inadmissible government that rules the Odonian society by stifling the individual mind" (147). Shevek's transformation into a social reformer is painful. "That the walls of his hard puritanical conscience were widening out immensely was anything but a comfort. He felt cold and lost. But he had nowhere to retreat to, no shelter, so he kept coming farther out into the cold, getting farther lost" (154). The renewal of his promise to his society is what he needs to counteract the dis-ease he feels in his propertarian relationship with Sabul.

Takver gives Shevek the name of what he needs to counteract his parents' broken promise, "the bond," partnering, "body and mind all the years of life" (160). When Takver tells Shevek that the relationship she needs with him in this promise of lifelong fidelity, he recognizes his reciprocal need: "He had a feeling of un-limitedness, of clarity, total clarity, as if he had been set free" (160). As the walls of his personal and social relationships are pushed back, Shevek sees the connection between his unified concept of time and the events in his own life. The promise is the human act that combines time, responsibility, and morality. The bond with Takver becomes Shevek's model for human relationships.

Le Guin emphasizes the tenuousness of Shevek's achievements in the alternate chapters (1, 3, 5, 7), which show the older Shevek on Urras moving in the opposite direction, from an expanded sense of intellectual stimulation and of love for the parent country to a sense of being isolated and walled in.

The novel opens with Shevek's ten-day space voyage to and arrival on Urras. This experience is a microcosm of his whole Urrasti experience and the challenge of working in an archist state. Shevek's first challenge is alienation. In the confusion and disorientation of seeing his world drop out from under him, he momentarily believes he has forfeited his "birthright of decision" (8), free choice. Further, his conversations with the Urrasti physician on the ship bring him in contact with the mental walls which keep the Urrasti from questioning their assumptions about human nature and the relationship between individual and society. A second challenge is that of assimilation. At the end of his first day on Urras, Shevek says to his colleagues in physics. "You have your anarchist. What are you going to do with him?" (22). Shevek intends it as an ironic remark, but it is more ironic than he realizes. Having brought him to Urras to do the kind of physics that they need to enhance their own power, the Urrasti indeed do "have" Shevek; they have "bought" him, and he will have to confront his coopting before he is free to return to Anarres.

Le Guin thus brings her utopist up against the walls of the state, walls that create a reality which includes prisons, class structure, sexism, and armies. The promise, that most essential of all personal and social relationships, is here denigrated to a social amenity, as when Vea asks Shevek, "Will you call me? Promise?" (178). The Urrasti question about the Anarresti, "What keeps people in order?" (132), is an example of what the Gethenian Foretellers in *The Left Hand of Darkness* would have called the wrong question, for behind it is the assumption that people need an external authority to make them do that which is in the best interest for the continuation of society. Shevek's answer begins with his assertion that basically "people like to do things. They like to do them well." He continues:

It is the question of ends and means. After all, work is done for the work's sake. It is the lasting pleasure of life. The private conscience knows that. And also the social conscience, the opinion of one's neighbors. There is no other reward, on Anarres, no other law. One's own pleasure, and the respect of one's fellow. That is all. When that is so, then you see the opinion of the neighbors becomes a very mighty force (133).

As an anarchist Shevek wants to unbuild walls, but the Urrasti are determined to reinforce the walls that will make clearer their own uniqueness and superiority among the known worlds. To get what they want they are willing to move the wall out far enough to include Shevek and, in using the phrase "we Cetians," to include Anarres itself, at least in name. To resist becoming their pawn Shevek must learn to distrust others and wall himself off from their power. He discovers, however, that he is then capable of acting like a Urrasti. At Vea's party he becomes drunk, forces himself on Vea, and tries to dominate others with his arguments about the superiority of Anarres.

For all the walls he sees around him, still it is on Urras that Shevek finds the intellectual stimulation to do physics. In fact, at Vea's party he meets nonphysicists who are more curious about his work than most Anarresti ever were. Their conversation provides the essential concepts for understanding the connection between Shevek's physics and the ethics of the Odonian promise. The discussion is strategically placed in the novel, for the next two chapters, 9 and 10, are the climaxes of Shevek's two journeys.

To explain the two aspects of time Shevek uses linear and cyclical metaphors:

Well, you know we think that the whole universe is a cyclic process, an oscillation of expansion and contraction, without any before or after. Only *within* each of the great cycles, where we live, only there is there linear time, evolution, change. So then time has two aspects. There is the arrow, the running river, without which there is no change, no progress, or direction, or creation. And there is the circle or the cycle, without which there is chaos, meaningless succession of instants, a world without clocks or seasons or promises (198).

His comments prompt one of the men to speculate that temporal physics could be applied to ethics. Although Shevek's explanation is lengthy, it needs to be quoted because it shows the connection between his professional work and his personal and social commitments:

Chronosophy does involve ethics. Because our sense of time involves our ability to separate cause and effect, means and end. . . . Seeing the difference between *now* and *not now*, we can make the connection. And there morality enters in. Responsibility. . . . To break a promise is to deny the reality of the past; therefore it is to

deny the hope of a real future. If time and reason are
functions of each other, if we are creatures of time, then
we had better know it, and try to make the best of it.
To act responsibly (199).

Shevek has explained the ethical and temporal basis of the promise. To make a promise is to commit to a
relationship in the future, to shape the future; to abide
by a promise is to honor a commitment made in the
past.[32] Abiding by promises acknowledges the circle of
time, accounts for "why things also endure" (197).
Without the act of human fidelity life is meaningless, a
series of sequential events, an experience of "the incoherence of time" (110).

Le Guin has arranged the alternating chapters so
that climaxes of each journey are juxtaposed. By the end
of the Urras chapter 7 and the Anarres chapter 8,
Shevek's journeys of discovery have become increasingly difficult and dissatisfying. In neither country or
time period does he have both professional and social
freedom.

Chapters 9 and 10 climax the Urras and Anarres
journeys, respectively; together they function as a single climax of the novel, fusing the form and content.
The Urras journey is climaxed by Shevek's professional
breakthrough to the general temporal theory and by the
social breakthrough to the Urrasti revolutionaries. At
their demonstration Shevek offers the Ioti the open-
handed promise of Odonianism:

THE HAINISH WORLD

We know that there is no help for us but from one another, that no hand will save us if we do not reach out our hand. And the hand that you reach out is empty, as mine is. You have nothing. You possess nothing. You own nothing. You are free. All you have is what you are, and what you give" (264–65).

The answer of the Ioti government displays the same intolerance and power that Odo rebelled against two hundred years ago, in the form of attacking government forces who shoot off the hand of a man standing near Shevek.

The Anarres journey is climaxed less dramatically but no less significantly. Shevek renews his bond with Takver and announces his intention to start a printing syndicate for those scientific essays, musical compositions, and dramas which conventional syndicates have rejected. In both countries he asserts his right to work at what he does best, and he asserts his right to be free and responsible to human societies. Between his professional and social commitments Shevek has achieved integrity and integration.

Chapters 9 and 10 also climax the novel, for they fuse its form and content. What Shevek discovers and how he discovers it are analogues for the idea and the methodology of Odonianism and of Le Guin's storytelling. In temporal physics Shevek's accomplishment is to "provide a field in which the relation of the two aspects or processes of time could be understood" (198);

he unifies that which seems contradictory: sequency and simultaneity. This unity out of fragmentation is analogous to the accomplishment of Odo in her development of a society without government. Her general social theory explains a society which unifies integrity and integration; that is, it is a theory based on the coexistence of individual and society in which each is committed to the preservation of the other.

Le Guin uses the form of alternating chapters to give the reader the experience of achieving unity out of fragmentation, and to illustrate the sequency and simultaneity in a singe life by depicting what changes and what endures in Shevek's life. The recurring images of the wall and the cycle support these ideas. Le Guin uses the image of the wall to express the ambiguities of sequency, the sense that each moment must appear separate from another in order for it to be considered as an entity, and yet the understanding that if moments are walled off from each other, responsible thinking and action can be avoided. She uses the cycle to express the idea of change and duration, the belief that journeys outward must eventually entail a return to one's roots.

Both the form and content of this novel rely on the methodology of uncertainty. In physics, only when Shevek accepts the unprovability of the coexistence is he able to complete the general temporal theory: "In the region of the unprovable, or even the disprovable, lay the only chance for breaking out of the circle and going ahead. . . . By simply assuming the validity of real coexistence he was left free . . . to go ahead" (247).[33] Similarly, in chapter 10 Shevek's renewal of his Odonian promise, in the form of the Syndicate of the Initiative, is a going ahead on the basis of uncertainty. He is declaring his freedom from doing what the conventional social conscience expects him to do.

> Outside the locked room is the landscape of time, in which the spirit may, with luck and courage, construct the fragile, makeshift, improbable roads and cities of fidelity: a landscape inhabitable by human beings.
> It is not until an act occurs within the landscape of the past and the future that it is a human act. Loyalty, which asserts the continuity of past and future, binding time into a whole, is the root of human strength; there is no good to be done without it (295).

Appropriately, the last three chapters of the novel delineate the responsibilities that follow from the commitments Shevek has made in his personal, professional, and social life. They depict him "in the landscape of time."

In chapter 12, the last Anarres chapter, Shevek's commitment to do physics includes his involvement in the Syndicate of the Initiative and leads to his acceptance of the Ioti invitation to their university, where he will have the "equipment, . . . colleagues and students" (333) he desperately needs. Shevek cannot prevent the pain (anger, hatred, verbal abuse, ostracism) directed

toward his family, for pain is part of the human condition. He can, however, counterbalance it with his continued love for them; further, as M. Teresa Tavormina
has pointed out, the pain cannot be justified, but it can
be understood by identifying its origin.[34]

In chapter 11, when Shevek makes arrangements
with the Terran ambassador to give his general temporal theory simultaneously to all the known worlds, he
gives them the gift of sharing; he demonstrates that
exchanges between individuals or societies need not be
based on profit or power. If the Odonians are right that
the means are the ends, meaning in part that the value
and nature of an end or accomplishment cannot be
separated from the means used to achieve it, then
Shevek's sharing will influence the nature of the federation among the nine known Hainish worlds. He has set
the example of acting on the principle of cooperation,
not competition. Thus Le Guin accounts for the nature
of the Ekumen of *The Left Hand of Darkness,* four thousand years away, which administers the exchange of
good and knowledge but does not govern people.

The final chapter of the novel concerns Shevek's
three-day flight from Urras to Anarres. It is the beginning of a new journey; the home he is returning to has
changed in his absence, and the man who is returning
to it has also changed. In a world of change where humans bind past and future together by the promise
made in the face of uncertainty, the Odonians know
that "you *can* go home again, . . . so long as you under-

stand that home is a place where you have never been" (48). Significantly, the last chapter takes place entirely in space; neither the takeoff from Urras nor the landing on Anarres is depicted. Shevek, then, is "no place," and it is here that he makes his commitment, as an Odonian, to Ketho, a Hainishman.

Freedom and responsibility are the gifts Shevek offers to Ketho: "Once you walk through the wall with me, then as I see it you are one of us. We are responsible to you and you to us; you become an Anarresti, with the same options as all the others. But they are not safe options. Freedom is never very safe" (339). The human solidarity that Shevek had hoped to find with the Urrasti he unexpectedly finds with the Hainish. Shevek and Ketho exchange the phrase "We are the children of time" in Iotic and Pravic (339). The act is akin to the Odonian promise, the acknowledgment that human responsibility is a temporal relationship. Shevek thus brings another element of change into the Anarresti society, and the novel ends in the middle of another revolution of this utopia.

The ambiguity of the utopia continues through the novel's concluding chapter. Ketho's entry into Anarres is to be signaled by his crossing the wall at the Anarres spaceport; it is the same wall Shevek crossed, signaling his exit from Anarres. The traditional utopia has usually been a geographically isolated world, the assumption being that it must wall out the contamination and complexity of the rest of the world. Le Guin's ambiguous utopia now has an ambiguous wall in the sense that Shevek has breached it. He has left and returned, he is bringing in Anarres's first offworld visitor, and he has released his general temporal theory which will make possible the invention of the ansible and communication with other worlds.

The novel's form was generated in uncertainty, and it concludes in uncertainty. Le Guin used the science fiction thought experiment as the basis of the novel, a method which does not provide certainty but does provide speculation. Her creative journey is like Shevek's: "It is not the answer we are after, but only how to ask the question" (200).

Notes

1. Le Guin, "Escape Routes," *The Language of the Night*, ed. Susan Wood (New York: Putnam's, 1979) 203. See the following for compatible definitions: H. Bruce Franklin, *Future Perfect: American Science Fiction of the Nineteenth Century* rev. ed. (Oxford: Oxford University Press, 1978) 3–4; Robert Scholes, *Structural Fabulation* (Notre Dame: University of Notre Dame Press, 1975); Darko Suvin, *The Metamorphoses of Science Fiction* (New Haven: Yale University Press, 1979) 7–8.

2. "Escape Routes" 206.

3. "Introduction to *The Left Hand of Darkness*," *Language of the Night* 156.

4. "Introduction to *The Left Hand of Darkness*" 155–56.

THE HAINISH WORLD

5. Le Guin, "Prophets and Mirrors: Science Fiction as a Way of Seeing," *Living Light* 7 (Fall 1970) 113.

6. "Introduction to *The Left Hand of Darkness*" 156.

7. Le Guin, *The Left Hand of Darkness* (New York: Harper & Row, 1980) 66.

8. Thomas J. Remington and Robert Galbreath, "Lagniappe: An Informal Dialogue with Ursula K. Le Guin," *Selected Proceedings of the 1978 Science Fiction Research Association National Conference* (Cedar Falls: University of Northern Iowa, 1979) 277–78.

9. James Bittner has charted the Hainish stories to show the relationship among their dates of composition, dates of publication, and dates in Hainish history; see his *Approaches to the Fiction of Ursula K. Le Guin* (Ann Arbor, MI: UMI Research Press, 1984) 91.

10. Brian Stapleford, "Galactic Empires," *The Science Fiction Encyclopedia*, ed. Peter Nicholls (Garden City, NY: Doubleday, 1979) 238–39. For a discussion of future history series in science fiction see Donald A. Wollheim, *The Universe Makers* (New York: Harper & Row, 1971).

11. Le Guin, "Is Gender Necessary? Redux," *Dancing at the Edge of the World* (New York: Grove, 1989) 16.

12. "Is Gender Necessary? Redux" 8, 10.

13. *The Left Hand of Darkness* 24. Subsequent references will be noted in parentheses.

14. Alfred Kroeber, "The Ancient Oikoumenê as a Historic Culture Aggregate," *The Nature of Culture* (Chicago: University of Chicago Press, 1952) 379–95.

15. Le Guin, "Winter's King," *The Wind's Twelve Quarters* (New York: Harper & Row, 1975) 106.

16. Le Guin, "Is Gender Necessary? Redux," *Dancing at the Edge of the World* 12.

17. For a discussion of the assertion that the novel is disunified, see David Ketterer, *New Worlds for Old: The Apocalyptic Imagination, Science Fiction and American Literature* (Bloomington: Indiana University Press, 1974) 76–90. For a discussion of the novel's unity see Martin

Bickman, "Le Guin's *The Left Hand of Darkness:* Form and Content," *Science-Fiction Studies* 4 (1977): 42–47. For criticism of the gender issues see Pamela J. Annas, "New Worlds, New Words: Androgyny in Feminist Science Fiction," *Science-Fiction Studies* 5 (1978): 143–56; and Joanna Russ, "The Image of Women in Science Fiction," *Red Clay Reader 7* (Charlotte, NC: Southern Review, 1970) 35–40.

18. Craig and Diana Barrow, "The Left Hand of Darkness: Feminism for Men," *Mosaic* 20 (1987): 84, 85.

19. For a discussion of the significance of the Foretelling episode see Anna Yaldine Clemens, "Art, Myth and Ritual in Le Guin's *The Left Hand of Darkness," Canadian Review of American Studies* 17 (1986): 423–36.

20. N. B. Hayles, "Androgyny, Ambivalence, and Assimilation in *The Left Hand of Darkness," Ursula K. Le Guin,* ed. Joseph D. Olander and Martin Harry Greenberg (New York: Taplinger, 1979) 109.

21. Hayles 114.

22. Le Guin, *The Word for World is Forest* (New York: Berkley, 1976) 72. Subsequent references will be noted in parentheses. For a different reading of Le Guin's language in the novel see Michael R. Collings, "Sentences and Structured Meaning: Ursula K. Le Guin's *The Word for World is Forest," Cuyahoga Review* 2 (Spring/Summer 1984) 45–59.

23. Le Guin, "Introduction to *The Word for World is Forest," Language of the Night* 152.

24. Gary K. Wolfe, *"The Word for World Is Forest," Survey of Science Fiction Literature,* ed. Frank N. Magill (Englewood Cliffs, NJ: Salem Press, 1979) 5: 2492–96.

25. Ian Watson, "The Forest as Metaphor for Mind: 'The Word for World is Forest' and 'Vaster than Empires and More Slow,'" *Science-Fiction Studies* 2 (1975): 231–37.

26. Le Guin cites J. A. Hadfield and William C. Dement as sources on dream research. See Le Guin, afterword, *Again, Dangerous Visions I,* ed. Harlan Ellison (Garden City, NY: Doubleday, 1972) 126.

THE HAINISH WORLD

27. Le Guin, "Science Fiction and Mrs. Brown," *Language of the Night* 111, 112.

28. Robert C. Elliott, *The Shape of Utopia: Studies in a Literary Genre* (Chicago: University of Chicago Press, 1970) 85. For additional discussions of the literary utopia see Kenneth Roemer, "Utopia Studies: A Fiction with Notes Appended," *Extrapolation* 25 (1984): 318–34; Darko Suvin, "Science Fiction and Utopia Fiction: Degrees of Kinship," *Positions and Presuppositions in Science Fiction* (Kent, OH: Kent State University Press, 1988) 38.

29. Le Guin, "A Non-Euclidean View of California as a Cold Place to Be," *Dancing at the Edge of the World* 90.

30. Le Guin, headnote, "The Day Before the Revolution," *Wind's Twelve Quarters* 285. The four writers named are Percy Bysshe Shelley, Peter Kropotkin, Emma Goldman, and Paul Goodman. For an overview of anarchism see George Woodcock, "Anarchism," *Encyclopaedia Britannica: Macropedia*.

31. Le Guin, *The Dispossessed: An Ambiguous Utopia* (New York: Harper & Row, 1974) 40. Subsequent references will be noted in parentheses.

32. This discussion has been influenced by M. Teresa Tavormina's perceptive discussion of the physics in the novel: "Physics as Metaphors: The General Temporal Theory in *The Dispossessed*," *Mosaic* 13 (1980): 51–62. Generally helpful is a work Le Guin has cited: J. T. Fraser, ed. *The Voices of Time* (New York: Braziller, 1966).

33. Shevek's method of proceeding from intuition to scientific proof is similar to Gödel's procedure which led him to the Incompleteness Theorem. See Douglas R. Hofstadter, *Gödel, Escher, Bach: an Eternal Golden Braid* (New York: Basic Books, 1979) 15–19.

34. Tavormina 58.

CHAPTER FOUR

Orsinia

The imaginary Central European country of Orsinia has stimulated Ursula K. Le Guin's creativity longer than any of her other invented worlds. She began her publishing career in Orsinia, and she has returned to it after Earthsea and the Hainish planets, which established her reputation, appear to be closed to her imagination. Of Earthsea she said that once the protagonist Ged disappeared, she no longer had a guide in that country and could write no more Earthsea stories.[1] Of the Hainish planets she has recently stated that outer space journeys no longer interest her.[2]

In the first of her rare autobiographical essays Le Guin notes that prior to the publication of her first science fiction in 1962 she had written four novels "set in an invented though nonfantastic Central European country, as were the best short stories I had done."[3] Although apparently none of these novels has been published, Le Guin's first published poem (1959) and short story (1961) were Orsinian pieces.[4] Furthermore, it is in the Orsinian fiction that Le Guin mastered her craft. She once commented that when in her early twenties she finished the Orsinian story "A Week in the Country," she felt she had finished her apprenticeship.[5] After publishing individual Orsinian stories in the 1970s, she brought out a collection of short stories in 1976, *Orsinian Tales,* which was nominated for the National Book Award in 1977. She published an Orsinian novel, *Malafrena,* in 1979 and more short stories in the 1980s, primarily in *The New Yorker.*

The Orsinian pieces are essentially historical fiction in that they describe the matrix of a culture in a time prior to the years in which the stories were published. Le Guin has acknowledged their "literary origin" as being "the Russian novel . . . Tolstoy and Dostoyevsky."[6] What is intriguing about Le Guin's continued interest in Orsinia is that her own Hainish works reveal her awareness of modern physics and mathematics where the theories of relativity and probability have shaped a world view radically different from that of the eighteenth and early nineteenth centuries, when time and space were regarded as absolutes and when historical fiction was the dominant expression of this world view.

The great historical novelists of the nineteenth century tried to represent their empirical environment and reconstruct the details of the past, as Sir Walter Scott did with Norman England or Leo Tolstoy did with Russia in the Napoleonic era. Like other twentieth-century writers, well aware of the difficulty of defining "represent" in the absence of an objective reality, Le Guin uses the technique of distancing or estrangement to separate herself from the world of recorded history and to call attention to recorded history as a subjective construct.

Estrangement is a literary device by which the reader experiences a "radical discontinuity" between the world of consensus reality and the world in the fiction.[7] Although all fictional worlds are in some way different from the reader's world, estranged fictional worlds are radically different in physical location, history, or world view. What distinguishes Orsinia from Le Guin's fantasy and science fiction worlds is that it can be located in Europe in the distant and near past of Western civilization. Since the Orsinian fiction predates her science fiction and fantasy, it was in its creation that Le Guin first recognized the need to distance herself from consensus reality. As she notes in a recently published interview:

I was in college when I started the pieces that eventually became the *Orsinian Tales*. . . . I was stuck in that old formula . . . to write about what you know, what you've experienced. . . . I remember thinking finally, "To hell with it, I'll just make up a country." And since most of what I knew came out of books . . . I made up a place that was like the places in books I liked to read. But as soon as I began work in Orsinia, I realized I didn't have to imitate Tolstoy. I had created a place I could write about in my own terms; I could make up just enough of the rules to free my imagination and my observations.[8]

Le Guin develops Orsinia with the specific detail that readers expect in her fiction. She provides history, geographical features, names of places and people from a nonexistent language, and details of the daily lives of varied characters. In contrast to this world that has no referent in the reader's consensus reality are references to familiar events from European history such as Neville Chamberlain's 1938 meeting with Hitler in Munich, the October 1956 revolution in Hungary, the practice of tatooing numbers on the arms of prisoners in German work camps. Orsinia becomes a unique place with a unique history which is and is not continuous with consensus reality.

Used in the Orsinian fiction, estrangement calls attention to the subjective nature of history. Although modern historians may agree that a certain event happened during a given year and in a given area, they recognize that an account of the event and an estimate of its historical significance is unavoidably an interpretation. By writing about an imaginary country but embedding it in the history of Central Europe, Le Guin has, in a sense, written an alternative history of Central Europe, particularly in *Orsinian Tales*, which will be the focus of this chapter.

Malafrena, even though published after *Orsinian*

Tales, provides geographic and political background for the tales. Told from the viewpoint of the landed gentry, the novel depicts Orsinia in the early nineteenth century, caught up in the idealism and fervor that followed the French Revolution and in the desire for independence that followed the Congress of Vienna in 1815. The novel focuses on Itale Sorde as he develops into a political revolutionary, having left his father's lands and gone to Krasnoy, the capital city. From 1825 to 1831 Sorde and his friends become more outspoken in their challenge to the Austrian Empire's right to rule Orsinia and in their call for the restoration of Orsinia's constitutional monarchy. Sorde, in both his political and personal life, fights for self-determination and independence.

In pursuit of the ideal he adopts a motto from the French debates, "Live free or die." However, his own imprisonment, the suicides of friends, his lover's insincere liberalism, and a failed insurrection eventually bring him home to heal both body and spirit. His belief in Orsinia's independence remains, but he has experienced the gulf between idealism and achievement. Le Guin has stated that she worked on the ideas and the story for twenty years, trying to get it right.[9] *Malafrena* does not reach the unity and complexity of *Orsinian Tales*, which both presents and questions history.

ORSINIA

Narrative Sequence

The narrative sequence that Le Guin uses in *Orsinian Tales* begins to define what the nature of Le Guin's alternative history is. Individual stories generally are told chronologically, but the arrangement of the eleven stories is nonchronological. Ranging from 1150 to 1965, the stories are arranged in the following order: 1960, 1150, 1920, 1920, 1956, 1910, 1962, 1938, 1965, 1640, 1935.

James Bittner has suggested that the arrangement, a moving backward and then forward in time, reflects the circular romance quest which he has argued is the aesthetic structure of Le Guin's fiction. The quest proceeds by "returns which are also advances."[10] The circular quest takes on additional significance when one tries to understand Le Guin's concept of history. The nonchronological order of the collection coupled with the chronological order within individual stories reveal that Le Guin's historical fiction is, like her science fiction, based on the perception of time as both succession and duration. *Orsinian Tales* is a more complex book than *Malafrena* because it offers the experience of this double vision of time.

Although a unified theory of time, such as Shevek discovered in *The Dispossessed*, does not yet exist, many writers—most recently Stephen Jay Gould in *Time's Arrow, Time's Cycle*—have argued for the necessity of viewing time both ways. Time as succession, often imaged as the arrow or river, is the perception of time as a series of moments, each separate and unrepeatable. This perception explains change and is experienced in people's conscious, daily activities. Time as sequence is the basis of narration, that powerful order used to make sense out of both fact and fiction. On the other hand, time as duration, often imaged as the cycle, is the perception of time as fundamental states which are always present or regularly repeated. This perception explains changelessness and connectedness; humans experience it in dreams and myths. Time as duration is the basis of immanence or a lawlike structure, that equally powerful structure used to account for a meaning beyond human existence.[11]

Le Guin's temporal physicist Shevek recognizes the apparent contradiction of the two views of time but argues for the necessity of both: "There is the arrow, the running river, without which there is no change, no progress, or direction, or creation. And there is the circle or the cycle, without which there is chaos, meaningless succession of instants, a world without clocks or seasons or promises."[12]

One of Le Guin's sources for her understanding of modern speculation about time is *The Voices of Time*, edited by J. T. Fraser. In his essay "Time as Succession and the Problem of Duration" in this collection Friedrich Kümmel argues that the acceptance of both perceptions is the only assurance for free and responsible actions. He writes:

No act of man is possible with reference solely to the past or solely to the future, but is always dependent on their interaction. Thus, for example, the future may be considered as the horizon against which plans are made, the past provides the means for their realization, while the present mediates and actualizes both. . . . This interrelation of reciprocal conditions is a historical process in which the past never assumes a final shape nor the future ever shuts its doors. Their essential interdependence also means, however, that there can be no progress without a retreat into the past in search of a deeper foundation.[13]

In *Orsinian Tales* the reader is challenged to "make sense" out of the obvious violation of the familiar chronological sequence. As the reader moves through the collection, the recurring question is, What does this story have to do with the preceding one? Thus, the reader's understanding of the text and of the Orsinian people becomes an accumulative experience; each story is reinterpreted as the next one is read. The reader not only experiences linear time (in each story and in the process of reading) but also cyclical time (for example, in relating a 1960 story to an 1150 story, and then both to a 1920 story).

The placement of the date at the end of each story suggests that the date is less important than what precedes it. The story's relationship to the other stories rests less on what is datable and more on what is repeated, such as themes, images, characters, places. The skewed chronological order reveals that Orsinia is all of these things and all of these people. A chronological sequence would encourage the reader to apprehend Orsinia only in the reductive, causal mode; the events of the 1150 story would be read as the "causes" of what occurred in later Orsinian history. Coherence would be dependent on sequency; unity would develop from simplicity rather than from multiplicity.

The reader views Orsinia within the framework of Western civilization as well as within the chronological history of Central Europe. As if trying to express her sense of her own European heritage, which was closely tied to German and Polish culture and to specific locations, Le Guin named her country after herself. James Bittner explains, "The country's name ... and its creator's name have the same root: *orsino,* Italian for 'bearish,' and *Ursula* come from the Latin *ursa.*"[14] Furthermore, the Russian invasion of Czechoslovakia in 1947 was a traumatic political event for Le Guin. She wrote, "That's when I came of age, and realized I had a stake in this world. . . . Writing about Orsinia allowed me to talk about a situation that had touched my heart, yet I could distance it, which was very important at that time."[15]

With such countries now known as Hungary, Czechoslovakia, Poland, Rumania, and Yugoslavia, Orsinia has shared medieval feudalism and the long struggle for independence. Central Europe has a long

ORSINIA

history of invasion, war, and oppression. Because it lacks major geographic borders, it has been overrun by its strong neighbors, Turkey in the South, Central Asia to the East, and Germanic tribes to the west. Orsinia shares with other European countries the dream of liberty that triggered the French Revolution. Not only did Napoleon march across it to invade Russia in 1812, opposing forces fought major battles of both world wars on its soil. The desire for political autonomy is evident in the uprisings, strikes, and revolutions of the last thirty years. The cost of imperialism is evident in the daily lives of the Orsinians.

The efficacy of Le Guin's technique of using both linear and cyclic sequence can be demonstrated by examining the first three stories in *Orsinian Tales.* "The Fountains," "The Barrow," and "Ile Forest," dated 1960, 1150, and 1920 respectively, introduce the reader to Le Guin's concept of history and the texture that is Orsinia. Each protagonist is different, but each faces choices which change his sense of who he is and what his commitments are to the human community, seen as Orsinia, one's immediate neighbors, or a particular geographic area.

"The Fountains" tells of the defection by a renowned Orsinian microbiologist attending an international conference in Paris. Although heavily shadowed by secret police, he suddenly finds, during a tour of Versailles, that he is alone. As he walks away from the fountains and into the estate forest, he gradually realizes that he must decide whether to become a permanent exile or return to his Parisian hotel, a symbolic return to Orsinia. To seek asylum in one of the foreign embassies in Paris will give him security, but he will be forever locked out of Orsinia. To return to the hotel will be a free choice to return home, but he will be again under the scrutiny of a willful government. Standing on the Solferino Bridge in Paris, near midnight, he makes his choice: "But he had never cared much about being safe, and now thought that he did not care much about hiding either, having found something better: his family, his inheritance. . . . What turned him to his own land was mere fidelity. For what else should move a man, these days?"[16]

There could hardly be a stronger contrast than to move from the humane love which Dr. Adam Kereth feels for his European ancestors and his Orsinian fellow citizens to the fear and guilt of Count Freyga in "The Barrow" which cause him to sacrifice a visiting priest and then establish and defend a Benedictine monastery in his province. Freyga's province is Montayna, a mountainous isolated region inhabited by Orsinian Christians and heathen barbarians. Freyga, twenty-three years old, count since barbarians killed his father three years ago, has his ears filled with his wife's cries from upstairs as she labors in childbirth. He fears for the life of his seventeen-year-old wife, and the winter darkness that fills the downstairs hall makes him suspicious of the foreign priest from the city. Overcome by his fears and

ORSINIA

suspicions, Freyga takes the priest to the heathen barrow, slits his throat, and disembowels him. Later that
night when he sees his wife and son safe and well, he
kneels by the bed and murmurs, "Lord Christ, be
praised, be thanked" (13). Torn by conflicting belief systems, the count has tried to appease both gods.

In the context of the first two stories, the trade
of death for life is seen as a universal human response.
In the background of "The Fountains" is the opulence
of Versailles, one cause of the French Revolution, which
was followed by republican and then imperialistic blood-
baths, deaths traded for life and power. In the background of "The Barrow" is Christianity, which begins
with the sacrifice of Jesus so that his followers might
have life everlasting. Horrible as Freyga's action is, it
must be viewed as an act which may be the foundation
for a religion or a government, as plausible a foundation
as Kereth's act of fidelity.

"Ile Forest" is also a story about killing. The story
of Galven Ileskar is told by a senior physician in response to his younger partner's unqualified assertion
that "murder can't go unpunished" (15). Although he
has no memory of it, Ileskar, in a fit of jealous rage,
killed his wife and her lover; he lives in "a half-ruined
house at the end of nowhere" (23), a self-imposed exile
in punishment for what he cannot remember. The storyteller and his sister meet Ileskar when the physician
comes to practice in the village; the only person who
knows of Ileskar's deed is Martin, his hired man. When

the sister falls in love with Ileskar, the physician, dis-
turbed over Ileskar's passivity and isolated life style,
forces the story out of Martin. The physician fears for
his sister's well-being and tells her the story. Un-
daunted, experiencing "the sense of peril, which is the
root of love" (24), she marries Ileskar. Ileskar is capable
of passionate rage and gentle love; he acted out the dark
side of himself one time in his life, but it was so horrible
to his more rational, ethical self that he can no longer
remember the act. However, he is very aware of the
absence of something in his memory, and it is that
awareness of absence that makes him capable of love
and gentleness.

As different as these three protagonists are, they
represent the range of human emotion for fidelity, love,
rage, fear. By violating the chronological order Le Guin
helps the reader recognize the universal in the particular; if these stories had been arranged in chronological
order ("The Barrow," "Ile Forest," "The Fountains"),
the reader might think of Freyga as only the predecessor
of Ileskar and be so overwhelmed with these accounts
of murder that the love and fidelity of Kereth for his
compatriots would seem incredible or inconsequential.
Furthermore, having experienced the significant act of
fidelity by Kereth at the beginning, the reader recognizes that Freyga and Ileskar also share this quality.

Both the protagonists and the readers discover that
rethinking the past allows them to understand who they
are and what their commitments and responsibilities

will be to their geographic area and its human community. Without this reassessment, the individual would be imprisoned by the past, blindly committed to something not understood.

By insisting on a double vision of time—as both linear and cyclic—Le Guin refuses to privilege chronological order either in constructing history or in constructing fiction. Implicit in this collection of short stories is an examination of how historical fiction is made meaningful, and Le Guin both uses and calls into question the chronological beginning, middle, and end structure of a narrative.

By not following chronological order for the arrangement of the stories in the collection, Le Guin deemphasizes the beginning and end and emphasizes the middle. The first and the last stories are significant more for the ideas, themes, and images they share with the other stories than as an account of origin and resolution. They do function as a beginning and ending of the reading process for the audience by offering a way into and then out of Orsinia. The collection begins with "The Fountains," the only story set outside of Orsinia. When Dr. Kereth decides not to defect, the reader's attention and curiosity turn to Orsinia. The collection ends with "Imaginary Countries," the only story in which the omniscient narrator speaks to the reader. At the end of the story the narrator comments, "But all this happened a long time ago, nearly forty years ago; I do not know if it happens now, even in imaginary countries" (179).

UNDERSTANDING URSULA K. LE GUIN

The selection of the first and last stories, then, is certainly not arbitrary; but at the same time the selection is not decisive. Rather, these two stories suggest a tentative beginning and ending; the reader could begin to reread the stories, following a circular pattern rather than a linear one, with the end blurring into the beginning. The reader could, using the dates, reread the stories in chronological order; "The Fountains" would become the ninth story, "Imaginary Countries" would become the middle story, "The Barrow" would be the first, and "The House" would be the last. A reexamination of the collection reveals other tentative qualities. The chronology of Orsinia is full of gaps, as the dates emphasize: 1150, 1640, 1910, 1920, 1935, 1938, 1956, 1960, 1962, 1965. The title *Tales* suggests an oral origin and the possibility that each is only one version of an oft-repeated story. The word *tale* is a more general term than *story* and may be applied to a narrative account of either fact or fiction. Furthermore, the omniscient narrator has stepped into the collection at the end of the last story as if for the sole purpose of qualification: "I don't know if it happens now."

Individual stories generally follow chronological order, but they also call attention to the importance of the middle. Although they too have functional beginnings and endings, because they are not preceded or followed by stories which are chronologically related to them their beginnings and endings are inconclusive. The ending is always open in that the story ends just as the protagonist begins to live with a new view of self, work, and human community. Usually the protagonist does not fully understand the implications of the new awareness; furthermore the story ends with unanswered or even unanswerable questions. Thus the middle is more significant than the beginning or the ending.

In the third story Le Guin suggests this emphasis on the middle. Nearing the end of his story, the senior physician says of his sister,

"But my telling her forced her to take sides. And she did. She said she'd stay with Ileskar. They were married in October."
The doctor cleared his throat, and gazed a long time at the fire, not noticing his junior partner's impatience.
"Well?" the young man burst out at last like a firecracker—"What happened?"
"What happened? Why, nothing much happened" (28–29).

And then the physician tells his audience of the uneventful, happy years of Ileskar and his wife. The listener's question, "What happened?" implies that he is most interested in the outcome, perhaps expecting another murder. The storyteller, however, is absorbed in the events of the story, the process of living.

The suggestions of tentativeness and of things blurring into one another reinforce the idea that the structure of a historical narrative for Le Guin cannot be only the chronological beginning-middle-end but must also be a revolving spiral; all aspects of the narrative develop a central theme and examine it both in linear and in cyclic relationship to other things. In a 1980 essay on narration Le Guin used such a structure and quoted a description of it as "radial, circling about, repeating and elaborating the central theme. It is all middle."[17] Apparent discontinuity, then, becomes continuity.

Le Guin's narrative structure in *Orsinian Tales* is consistent with a world view shaped by modern physics. Her account of Orsinia has neither beginning nor end nor completeness, for the present is ongoing, the past is always being reinterpreted, and the future is open. The individual life, the history of Orsinia, and the narrative gain meaning not merely by the nature of beginning or end but by the quality of the middle.

Unifying Theme

The collection of stories is further unified by a central theme that defines the quality of life. The history of Orsinia that is retold in these eleven tales reveals that in a world of change, catastrophe, and indeterminacy, Orsinians have survived and maintained some sense of integrity and self-worth by personal vows of fidelity. Le Guin's characters, settings, plots, resolutions, and images reflect the power of this moral principle. The principle may be called commitment, love, comradeship, or fidelity; regardless of its name, adherence to it provides constancy in a world of inconstancy. Le Guin makes very clear that constancy results from individual choices. Fidelity is the central theme around which the stories circle, "repeating and elaborating" its implications for individuals and for the country. One of her characters sings:

> Yet be just and constant still, Love may beget a wonder,
> Not unlike a summer's frost or winter's fatal thunder:
> He that holds his sweetheart dear until his day of dying
> Lives of all that ever lived most worthy the envying (120).

The first three stories of the collection depict characters facing unexpected events and "fatal thunder" in Kereth's opportunity to defect, Count Freyga's need to save the lives of his wife and unborn child, the listener's discovery that a murderer can also be a brother. In each life meaningfulness resulted from how the characters reacted to these events. In keeping with Le Guin's emphasis on indeterminacy, however, each story ends with unanswered questions about the characters' future; there can be no "finished version" of a life.

The matrix of each story contains several elements that heighten the immediacy of change. As James Bittner has indicated, the karst area, which is the setting for "Brothers and Sisters," is a reminder of the natural change occurring in the land itself. Karst is a limestone area where water action underground produces caverns, sinkholes, and underground streams. Further, almost all of the stories take place in the fall, October frequently being mentioned—"the month when things fall," Le Guin once called it.[18] The equally constant and immanent change in the human world is emphasized by ruins and remnants of human things. The barrow is an abandoned altar of the barbarians, the top stone of which has become the altar in the nearby church. The count's tower is glimpsed in "A Week in the Country" by its 1962 protagonists as "the ruins of the Tower Keep." The family house in which the protagonist of "The House" was born and in which he lived with his wife for several years is empty, abandoned even by the government which once used it for offices. The people themselves are often maimed or scarred. These injuries, often a result of war or revolution, are a constant reminder of the cost of the struggles for autonomy in this landlocked Central European country.

Le Guin uses the image of the road to suggest the immediacy of change and the opportunity for either escape or action that may improve the future of an individual or of Orsinia. Hope, she shows, is based on a belief in the openness of the future, which in turn is based on learning from the past. In "The Road East," a story of events in October 1956, Le Guin recounts a few days in a young man's life when he is faced with the conflicting fidelities of commitment to his mother, who denies the existence of evil, and commitment to his friends and fellow Orsinians who are risking their lives to plan a revolution.

Maler Eray's technique for coping with the growing tension is to imagine walking eastward from Krasnoy to Sorg, a journey, he imagines, to a secure city, "early in the last century" (62). Although in his imagination he can reject the idea that "home" must always be with his mother, he cannot act on this desire. In contrast to his mother, who lives literally and figuratively behind a closed door, tending her flowers and blithely announcing, "nothing is evil, nothing is wasted, if only we look at the world without fear" (66), is a woman who is identified with the road. An enigmatic figure, almost at times seeming to be a figment of his imagination, she serves as a guide for Eray. For she has come from Sorg, walking west on the road which Eray had always thought of as "the road east." She makes Eray think about going in a different direction, about accepting the responsibility his friend Provin had held out to him: "There's nothing left to us, now, but one another" (64). Realizing he cannot escape to the country, or to the past, Eray acts. He leaves his mother, "dazzled at first by the bright October sunlight, to join the army of the unarmed and with them to go down the long streets leading westward to, but not across, the river" (70).

The closing words provide knowledge of Eray's newly pledged fidelity, but they give no certainty that he will even survive the revolution. Eray has created

UNDERSTANDING URSULA K. LE GUIN

an open future because he has relinquished his concept of the past as a fixed condition and because he decides that his actions are meaningful for himself and for Orsinia.

Just as the road serves as a symbol of change, the house often serves as a symbol of duration. "A Week in the Country" uses both of these symbols in an account of coming-of-age experience for a university student from Krasnoy in 1962.

By taking the roads to the country, Stefan Kabbre encounters great change; he experiences familial love, vows fidelity that will lead to a marriage, sees his best friend shot by Orsinian soldiers, and endures torture and imprisonment. The Augeskar house in the country symbolizes the family unit and its regular summer gathering which reunites and nourishes them all. The autonomy symbolized by the house is a microcosm of that autonomy the country of Orsinia does not have. The unity and endurance of the family, however, is a microcosm of that unity and fidelity that Orsinians depend on for a sense of identity in spite of the domination of foreign powers.

Stefan is aware of being an outsider, not only because he is not one of the six Augeskar children, but also because his family is no longer intact. He relishes the memory of an April morning when he, his father, and his grandfather walked out on the karst plain so that the grandfather could vent his anger at being "yoked to the foreign plow" with no hope of aid from the West. While the grandfather talks, however, his hand rests on his grandson's shoulder, the tender touch conveying the values that remain, "obduracy" and "fidelity."

Stefan's memory takes him back to the past to recover that which is valuable, and the men's sharing with him their secret desires overshadows for Stefan the knowledge "that his grandfather had died in a deportation train and his father had been shot along with forty-two other men on the plain outside town in the reprisals of 1956" (116).

The reader's memory also brings back something valuable, the previous story. "Brothers and Sisters," which concerns events in 1910, is about Stefan's grandfather when the grandfather was twenty-three. The reader, from the privileged perspective of viewing the same struggle in two different generations of the same family, sees the stages of life repeated from one generation to another. In both narratives the coming-of-age experience involves, on the one hand, knowledge of one's own mortality and, on the other hand, knowledge of love, of the need to commit to other human beings. Both kinds of knowledge are essential to cross the threshold into adulthood, are essential to "sharing . . . the singular catastrophe of being alive" (73). "What is it all for?" the young man wonders, and the reader sees at least a partial answer; it is not the nature of one's birth or death which holds the answer but rather the middle, how one deals with death, fear of failure, injustice, irrational acts by others, love, self-definition, self-determination.

Stefan's coming-of-age experience has been traumatic; ironically, he has had to experience the very unknowns of life that he had once welcomed when they were only imagined. What were words in an intellectual argument at the beginning of the vacation are words of personal commitment at the end of the vacation: "No good letting go." Like Maler Eray's experience in "The Road East," Stefan's guide to action is a woman. Bruna is representative of many of the women in the Orsinian stories. Like Tenar in *The Tombs of Atuan* they often choose the more difficult road and guide their male companions on it.

In "An die Musik," the next story, another way of coping with being borne down by oppressive human acts is offered. This story focuses on a music composer in 1938 who, hearing the radio news reports that suggest impending world war, wonders about the value of his life's task, which is to write a Mass. He is advised to write short songs that can be performed immediately. He is told, "This is not a good world for music . . . when Europe is crawling with armies like a corpse with maggots, when Russia uses symphonies to glorify the latest boiler-factory in the Urals. . . . Music is no good, no use. . . . Write your songs, write your Mass, it does no harm. . . . But it won't save us" (140). He chooses to fulfill two vows of fidelity which will conflict in their demands on his time. He cannot give up his commitment to the Mass, nor can he give up his commitment to his wife and children. Like Stefan Fabbre, who senses that the linear view of time is not the only way to regard history, Gaye is finally able to recognize that everything that is significant cannot be incorporated into a human history which is viewed as progress.

What good is music? None, Gaye thought, and that is the point. To the world and its states and armies and factories and Leaders, music says, "You are irrelevant"; and, arrogant and gentle as a god, to the suffering man it says only, "Listen." For being saved is not the point. Music saves nothing. Merciful, uncaring, it denies and breaks down all the shelters, the houses men build for themselves, that they may see the sky (144–45).

Music, or art in general, points to the presence of the world beyond human limits. As James Bittner explains, "The function of art . . . is to deny the world, to detach people from politics and history so they can receive visions of a better world, and perhaps redeem politics and history with that vision."[19]

In *Orsinian Tales* Le Guin has indeed written historical fiction that is consistent with a world view shaped by modern physics. The technique of estrangement calls attention to the subjective nature of history. The narrative sequence reveals her acceptance of both linear and cyclic time. Her account of Orsinia has neither beginning nor end nor completeness, for the present is ongoing, the past is always being reinterpreted, and the future is open. Finally, by using the theme of fidelity to unify the collection, she reveals that individuals find meaning and constancy in the face of change and impermanence by personal vows of commitment. The individual life, like the history of Orsinia, gains meaning not by the nature of its beginning or end but by the quality of the middle.

The closing lines of the collection leave the reader also in the middle of the narrative. The narrator writes, "But all this happened a long time ago, nearly forty years ago; I do not know if it happens now, even in imaginary countries." Not only does "this" refer to the eleventh story, it also refers to all the Orsinian tales. The reader then wonders just what has occurred in these stories. So the ending is not a closure but instead is an unanswered question that initiates rereading.

The rereading occurs with the reader puzzling over other unanswered questions. The doubt in the statement "I don't know if it happens" may be referring to the whole act of creating art. What if the art of storytelling is lost? What is art for? More particularly, Le Guin's narrator may be questioning whether or not stories like these can still be imagined, written, and published. Over Orsinia, Central Europe, and therefore over all the human family hangs the threat of additional imperialism and oppression, as well as the threat of atomic warfare. The reader hears the question, Can the author create in a world like this, create stories where

ORSINIA

commitment to each other is of the greatest value and where people accept both change and duration, reason and imagination, history and fiction?

Orsinian Tales is as open-ended a book as *The Dispossessed*, valued for the questions it raises and for not providing simple answers. The reader is left in the middle of both narratives, an experience Le Guin offers again in the most recent novel of her fourth world, the future American West Coast.

Notes

1. Thomas J. Remington and Robert Galbreath, "Lagniappe: An Informal Dialogue with Ursula K. Le Guin" *Selected Proceedings of the 1978 Science Fiction Research Association National Conference* (Cedar Falls: University of Northern Iowa, 1979) 279.

2. "Ursula K. Le Guin—Down to Earth," *Locus* Sept. 1984: 1.

3. Le Guin, "A Citizen of Mondath," *The Language of the Night*, ed. Susan Wood (New York: Putnam's, 1979) 28.

4. Le Guin, "Folksong from the Montayna Province," *Prairie Poet* Fall 1959: 75, and "An die Musik," *Western Humanities Review* 15 (1961): 247–58.

5. Conversation with Le Guin, The University of Chicago, (26–27 Oct. 1979).

6. Larry McCaffery and Sinda Gregory, "An Interview with Ursula Le Guin," *The Missouri Review* 7, No. 2 (1984): 71.

7. Robert Scholes, *Structural Fabulation: An Essay on Fiction of the Future* (Notre Dame: University of Notre Dame Press, 1975) 28. Darko Suvin was the first critic to explore the technique of estrangement in science fiction; see his *Metamorphoses of Science Fiction: On the Poetics*

and History of a Literary Genre (New Haven: Yale University Press, 1979).

8. McCaffery and Gregory, 71.

9. McCaffery and Gregory, 72.

10. James W. Bittner, *Approaches to the Fiction of Ursula K. Le Guin* (Ann Arbor, MI: UMI Research Press, 1984) 33.

11. Stephen Jay Gould, *Time's Arrow, Time's Cycle: Myth and Metaphor in the Discovery of Geological Time* (Cambridge, MA: Harvard University Press, 1987). See also Mircea Eliade, *The Myth of the Eternal Return* (Princeton: Princeton University Press, 1954).

12. Le Guin, *The Dispossessed: An Ambiguous Utopia* (New York: Harper & Row, 1974) 198.

13. Friedrich Kümmel, "Time as Succession and the Problems of Duration," *The Voices of Time,* ed. J. T. Fraser (New York: Braziller, 1966) 50.

14. Bittner 29.

15. McCaffery and Gregory 72.

16. Le Guin, *Orsinian Tales* (New York: Harper & Row, 1976) 4. Subsequent references will be noted in parentheses.

17. Le Guin, "It Was a Dark and Stormy Night; or, Why Are We Huddling about the Campfire?" *Dancing at the Edge of the World* (New York: Grove, 1989) 25.

18. Le Guin, "Coming of Age," *Wild Angels* (Santa Barbara: Capra Press, 1975) 14. October is also the month of Le Guin's birth.

19. Bittner 51.

CHAPTER FIVE

The West Coast

When *Always Coming Home* was published in 1985, a novel about people who "might be going to have lived a long, long time from now in Northern California,"[1] many readers felt Le Guin had created a new world. Actually the novel should be read in the context of a fourth world which she had been exploring since 1971—a future, reshaped American West Coast. Before 1985 Le Guin had published two works set in this world, the novel *The Lathe of Heaven* (1971) and the novella "The New Atlantis" (1975). In 1979 short stories began to appear which would eventually be published as part of *Always Coming Home*. The works set in this West Coast world share thematic concerns and genre; all are science fiction, and all posit a catastrophe that threatens the future of the American society.

In the Hainish novels outer space was a setting for the wide-ranging journey of discovery and the exploration of the diversity of the human community. On the coast, however, the journey stops, and assessment must occur; one can no longer follow the directive "Go West, young man, go West," an expression of the American dream of finding fortune, adventure, and fame in the New World. In a 1982 interview Le Guin stated: "One thing I've noticed about my settings is that when I have something I really don't want to say but which insists on being said I set it in Portland. *The Lathe of Heaven* and *The New Atlantis* are among the saddest things I've written, the nearest to not being hopeful, and they're both set right here. I don't know the reason for this."[2] Each time she reshapes the coast by natural or human disasters: pollution, wars, earthquakes, volcanic eruptions.

All three novels are set in the twenty-first century, and their plots depend on such sciences as psychology, anthropology, physics, geology, political science, and computer science. Further, they are all utopias or dystopias. Although Le Guin has continually carried on a quarrel with the concept of the planned utopia in her fiction, the fourth world is the only one where she overtly considers the issues in all of the works set there.[3] *The Lathe of Heaven* is a criticism of the planned utopia; "The New Atlantis" portrays a government-controlled society that has become a dystopia. *Always Coming Home* rejects the traditional utopia and offers an open-ended utopia.

These works are not unified by a common thought experiment as were the Hainish novels. Each is generated from its own thought experiment. Particular historical events do not appear in more than one novel, although the novels share the presence of an industrialized, capitalistic society that is self-destructive. These novels reflect Le Guin's concern with the shape of her world; behind them are events such as the extermination of California Indian tribes, the Jewish holocaust, Hiroshima with all its portents for a nonfuture, the Vietnam war, the cold war, and the arms race.

Like the science fiction of Philip K. Dick and Stanislaw Lem, Le Guin's West Coast novels question the nature of reality, particularly the view that knowledge of reality is acquired by reason. They posit a belief in the visionary world and in the value of mental activities such as intuition, imagination, and dreaming. These works become progressively more self-reflexive. They raise questions about the distinction between fact and fiction, imagination and reality. They are science fiction works which are, in part, about the value of building fictional worlds, especially utopias.

The Lathe of Heaven

Published in 1971, *The Lathe of Heaven* shows some affinity with the other two novels Le Guin had just finished: the middle Hainish novel, *The Word for World is Forest,* and the middle Earthsea novel, *The Tombs of Atuan.* As in *The Word for World is Forest* she explores the effective power of dreams. As in *The Tombs of Atuan* she creates a protagonist who, for the greater part of the novel, has lost the way. Like Tenar, George Orr feels alienated from himself, society, and his environment.

Published three years before *The Dispossessed: An Ambiguous Utopia*, *The Lathe of Heaven* is Le Guin's first novel-length exploration of utopia. In it she overtly satirizes the Western utopia, which hovers in the background of *The Dispossessed* as a model Odonianism has rejected.

The parameters of Le Guin's thought experiment include a self-destructive society, a man with the ability to change reality by his dreams, and a dream specialist who seizes the opportunity to shape a better world. The novel is set in Portland, Oregon, in 2002; pollution by industrial and military waste has upset the ecology; the polar caps are melting, the temperature is rising, many of the animal species have disappeared, the world is overpopulated, and the cities are overcrowded. The world is caught up in perpetual war, primarily being fought in Third World countries. The novel's protagonist is George Orr, an ordinary man who discovers he has the extraordinary ability to sometimes change reality with his dreams. The novel thus shifts through multiple "worlds," blurring the boundary between dreams and reality.

Orr's most traumatic dream and the one which left him unsure about whether he lived in dream-time or world-time was one he had in April 1998 when, during

THE WEST COAST

a nuclear attack on the United States, he saved the
world by dreaming into being a world without nuclear
war. Distraught over his uncontrollable power, he ob-
tained drugs to keep him from dreaming. Caught by the
police, he becomes a patient of Dr. William Haber, an
oneirologist or dream specialist.

Ostensibly trying to cure Orr, Haber begins directing Orr's dreams to create a better world. Haber is aided
by his invention, the Augmentor, a machine that can
record and stimulate brain activity. The dream sessions
between Haber and Orr become confrontational as Haber luxuriates in his power and his increasingly refined
record of Orr's brain waves. Away from Haber, Orr
gains support from Heather Lalache, the HEW lawyer
he has sought out to help protect his civil rights from
Haber, and from the Aliens of Aldebaran. Heather is
drawn to Orr's strength and stability, and the Aliens
have come to help because they recognize Orr as a great
dreamer.

Relying on the consistency gained by using the omniscient point of view and by focusing the majority of
chapters on Orr, Le Guin deftly takes the reader
through at least ten world changes. She develops the
novel as a series of meetings between Orr and Haber,
patient and therapist, dreamer and scientist, visionary
and rationalist, critic and utopist. Le Guin satirizes the
concept of the planned utopia by satirizing the attitudes
of one who sees himself capable of directing a planned
utopia. Haber has reduced his principles to three mot-

toes: The proper study of mankind is man; The greatest good for the greatest number; and The end justifies the means. Against these principles Orr argues that man is not the measure of all things; that if the single individual is not significant, nothing is; and that the means are the ends.

"The proper study of mankind is man," a line from Alexander Pope's *An Essay on Man,* is reinterpreted by Haber to mean that because humankind is superior to all other forms of existence in nature, only humankind needs to be studied. Haber asserts that man's purpose is "to do things, change things, run things, make a better world."[4] By replicating the capacity for effective dreaming, Haber believes he will be raising humankind to another evolutionary level; confidant, he cries out, "Then this world will be like heaven, and men will be like gods" (145).

George Orr rejects the idea that humankind is the measure of all things:

Things don't have purposes, as if the universe were a machine, where every part has a useful function. What's the function of a galaxy? I don't know if our life has a purpose and I don't see that it matters. What does matter is that we're a part. Like a thread in a cloth or a grass-blade in a field. It *is* and we *are*. What we do is like wind blowing on the grass (82).

THE WEST COAST

He has an instinctive sense of the play, the give-and-take between yin and yang, which constitutes the universe. Le Guin opens the novel with images of the experience of this play, of the pain that occurs when a disjunction occurs, and of one source of renewal. The "current-borne" jellyfish, "vulnerable and insubstantial," pulsing with the motions of the "moondriven sea," is like the human mind in dream or in vision, experiencing the balance of universal forces of which the individual is a part. Tossed onto the rocks and sand, "the terrible outerspace of radiance and instability," the creature is like "the mind . . . waking" to the difficulties of daily life, in which the "diurnal pulses" of the universe are not as readily felt (7). The passage suggests that one source for restoration of balance is in dreams. The dream, in that it puts a person in touch with the deepest levels of the psyche and with the collective unconscious, is both an experience of the relationship between part and whole on the psychic level and a metaphor for the relationship between part and whole on the cosmic level.

Unfortunately George Orr's world has such rough sand and rocks that his dreams become concerned with changing the world just so that the human community can survive. His dreams, therefore, do not give him either the psychic or the cosmic experience of balance. The title of the novel comes from a Taoist passage, placed as the headnote to chapter 3, that epitomizes Orr's attitude:

UNDERSTANDING URSULA K. LE GUIN

Those whom heaven helps we call the sons of heaven. They do not learn this by learning. They do not work it by working. They do not reason it by using reason. To let understanding stop at what cannot be understood is a high attainment. Those who cannot do it will be destroyed on the lathe of heaven (30).

All of the chapter headnotes, many from the texts of the two ancient Chinese Taoist philosophers Lao Tzu and Chuang Tzu, express the attribute of receptivity and the belief in nonrational modes (dreams, visions) as sources of knowledge. Orr is as recognizably Taoist as are Ged and Genly Ai. The difference is that Le Guin has created a protagonist who is not schooled as Ged is by the Masters and who is not familiar with Taoist principles as Ai is. To oppose the Faustian scientist Le Guin has selected the intuitive artist.

Orr wishes to adjust himself to the world; Haber wishes to adjust the world to the human race by means of technology. The two men, rationalist and dreamer, thus disagree on the nature of "proper study." Haber equates "studying" with "measuring"; he believes in the quantitative results of his machine. Haber consistently speaks of Orr's brain, not his mind, and explains Orr's effective dreams as a "complexly synchronized pattern of emissions that take ninety-seven seconds to complete itself and start again" (115). The dismissal of dreams by technologists as being "not real" is clearly satirized by Le Guin. The more numerical data that Haber collects from the machine he worships, the less he really understands about Orr.

Furthermore, Haber has masked his own emotional, intuitive, spiritual self. Denied normal outlets, it does not disappear but is displaced into Haber's irrational obsession for increasing his own power, for acquiring the ability to have effective dreams, and for his machine. Like Victor Frankenstein, Haber has become so obsessed with his research and his rationality that he has become irrational. His increasing insanity is akin to that of the country's leaders which led to the April 1998 world. Pollution, overpopulation, inequitable food distribution, and wars are destroying the world. Ethnocentrism and nationalism have led to the bizarre situation where protection of property and territory leads to their destruction. Orr compares the compartmentalization of Haber's mind to "politicians who sent the pilots to man the bombers to kill the babies to make the world safe for children to grow up in" (87).

The other two mottoes Haber uses to express his principles are corollaries of his particular interpretation of "The proper study of mankind as mind." Ethnically and epistemologically interested in goals and ends, he believes in "The greatest good for the greatest number" and "The end justifies the means."

The consequences of Haber's actions directed by these two principles are most shockingly manifested to Orr when Haber tries to solve the overpopulation of the world. Orr's effective dream is about a plague; so when

Haber wakes him the population of Portland has dropped from a million to a hundred thousand; the population of the world from seven billion to less than one billion. Horrified by the death of six billion people, Orr turns to Haber for an explanation. Haber replies breezily:

Was there any other solution, besides nuclear war? There is now no perpetual famine in South America, Africa, and Asia. When transport channels are fully re-stored, there won't be even the pockets of hunger that are still left. They say a third of humanity still goes to bed hungry at night; but in 1980 it was 92 per cent. There are no floods now in the Ganges caused by the piling up of corpses of people dead of starvation. There's no protein deprivation and rickets among the working-class children of Portland, Oregon (69).

Thus "the greatest number" which could lead a decent life on the planet has been achieved, and Haber can now, through Orr's dreams, improve the "goodness" of their lives.

The fulfillment of the greatest good for the greatest number depends on the actions of a director who can judge what is the greatest good. Le Guin uses the HURAD Tower in Portland, conjured up by Orr's un-conscious, as a symbol of Haber's view of himself and his relationship to the utopia he is making. The huge, towering structure from whose top floor Haber can look down upon the city reflects his desire for power and for distance between himself and the individuals whose lives he is affecting. Inside, the domed "immense black-marble foyer" (132) is analogous to the emptiness at the center of Haber's self. Orr is aware that "this building could stand up to anything left on Earth, except perhaps Mount Hood. Or a bad dream" (132). He thus names the two elements that threaten Haber's world: nature (the interrelated web of existence) and the nonrational forces of the human psyche, his own or Orr's.

In the end Haber's application of the principle that the end justifies the means leads to failure. He set out with a rational purpose but tapped the aid of the nonrational (Orr's dreaming) and treated it as if it operated rationally. Le Guin treats the failure of the dreams to achieve what Haber wanted them to with both humor and irony.

In contrast to Haber's desire to remake the world is Orr's desire to restore the balance between the human race and the environment so that humankind senses again the pulses of the universe, sees itself as "a thread in a cloth." In his increasingly assertive arguments with Haber, Orr acknowledges the value of some of Haber's achievements, but he reminds Haber of the cost of the progress. In response to Haber's catechism of data, Orr cries out, "But where's democratic government got to? People can't choose anything at all any more for themselves. Why is everything so shoddy, why is everybody so joyless?" (142).

Orr's invention of the Aliens can be seen as a desperate, nonrational response to Haber's dull world. They are nonaggressive, dreaming and dreamlike creatures who are, in a sense, a manifestation of the connection among all things that exist. If humans act as part of existence and not as dominator or conqueror, then the cosmic system is supportive of human existence, the future is inhabitable. Correspondingly, Orr's relationship with Heather Lalache epitomizes the bond within human community. As in most of Le Guin's science fiction, the paradigm of human society is the relationship between a man and a woman. Haber, however, has not achieved the balance of self and other which makes meaningful social relationships possible. Orr recognizes that Haber is insane: "He isn't in touch. No one else, no thing even, has an existence of its own for him; he sees the world only as a means to his end" (150).

In the concluding two and one-half chapters of the novel both Orr and the 2002 world escape from Haber's control. Orr's recovery is aided by "help from my friends." An Alien who owns an antique store gives Orr a record of "With a Little Help From My Friends"; Orr falls asleep listening to it and dreams Heather back into existence. In return, during the chaos that occurs when Haber hooks himself into the Augmentor and has an effective dream, Orr gives the world a "little help." He forces his way through a disintegrating world to Haber's tower and turns off the machine. Haber is last seen in a solitary room in the Federal Asylum for the Insane;

thin, unable or unwilling to communicate with anyone, he sat on the bed in his pajamas and "stared at the void" (171). His goal has been thwarted by the means he used to attain it, his own empty self.

Even though Orr was never able to convince Haber to change his views of reality, Haber's planned utopia has destroyed itself. In the postapocalyptic world that remains, "half wrecked and half transformed" (168), under the tutelage of one of the Aliens, Orr has become a designer of kitchen equipment, objects of balance and proportion and beauty. When he meets Heather for the first time in the new world, the Alien offers its final gift of words: "There is time. There are returns. To go is to return" (175).

In the context of Le Guin's continuing argument with the concept of utopia, *The Lathe of Heaven* is a story that, once written, need not be retold in other stories. She has effectively satirized the planned utopia, its godlike director, and its irrational dependence on reason; and she has effectively used the omniscient point of view to provide the larger perspective of utopist (Haber) and critics (Orr, Heather, and the Aliens). It is a significant step in Le Guin's search for a voice with which to discuss and shape a particular kind of utopia.[5]

The tension between the two world-builders, Orr and Haber, may well be a manifestation of a tension in Le Guin between the artist and the moralist. In her own world-building she must balance the rational, domineering, preaching self with the intuitive, patient, aesthetic self. Haber, in other words, may be an exaggeration of the didactic Le Guin who speaks in every novel but more obviously in *The Word For World is Forest* and in the two lesser works *Malafrena* and *The Eye of the Heron*. The tension becomes particularly great when she takes up the question of writing a literary utopia. Given her rejection of the planned and controlled utopia, how could she plan and create an alternative utopia without becoming a Haber-type utopist in the process? Is it possible to produce a genuine literary utopia? The novel's answer is duplicitous; Haber's utopia fails, but the novel is in the literary tradition of utopia.

"The New Atlantis"

"The New Atlantis" continues Le Guin's exploration of the concept of utopia and her search for the voice which could create a utopia. The setting is again Portland, Oregon, and its citizens are suffering from a ruined economy, pollution, overpopulation, depletion of natural resources, and excessive government control.

For several reasons the North American continent is sinking—continental shift, the melting of the polar ice caps due to the greenhouse effect, earthquake and volcanic activity on the West Coast and out on the Pacific Ocean floor. The latter activity causes an ancient people and their city to begin to rise toward the surface of the

THE WEST COAST

ocean. Le Guin tells her story through alternating sections; six sections are from the journal of Belle, a Portland woman, and six sections are told by the collective voice of the ocean people.

Belle's journal is an account of the descent of her world; she includes news reports about the continent sinking, and she summarizes her attempts to keep herself and her husband out of the grasp of government officials. Belle and her husband, Simon, are suspect because they are married, which is illegal, and because Simon's work in theoretical mathematics is in direct energy conversion, which could undermine the government's monopoly on power production and supply. Simon has just come home after eighteen months in a Rehabilitation Camp in Idaho. After twelve days he is taken away by the Bureau of Health, Education and Welfare; "since he was receiving Unemployment Compensation while suffering from an untreated illness, the government must look after him and restore him to health, because health is the inalienable right of the citizens of a democracy."[6] During his freedom Belle gets a black-market doctor and aspirin for him, plays her viola in the bathroom, where the FBI microphone is planted, to mask the clandestine meetings between her husband and a small group of scientists and engineers who have made a working solar cell. The greatest freedom they have is in imagining a better world.

One night Belle translates one of her visions into her music. Deeply moved, a mathematician exclaims,

"I saw it. I saw the white towers, and the water stream-
ing down their sides, and running back down to the
sea. And the sunlight shining in the streets, after ten
thousand years of darkness" (82). Even though none of
the group is able to act on their dreams, Belle's music
is active; it is a factor in the ascent of the city from the
ocean. The city's inhabitants have been awakened by a
change in pressure, and their sections of the story record their increased sensory awareness of light, time,
motion, sea creatures, and finally of sound, including "*a
huge, calling, yearning music from far away in the darkness*"
(75–76). They are also awakened internally: "We began
to remember," they frequently say.

The thought experiment behind these episodes in
two cities seems to be a working out of the political and
geologic consequences of the metaphor "the rise and
fall of nations." Like *The Lathe of Heaven* the story is
apocalyptic, an old world is exchanged for a new one.

Charlotte Spivack has shrewdly asked which city
the title refers to. Is America the new Atlantis in that it
is sinking into the sea, or is the ocean city the new
Atlantis in that it is the old Atlantis coming into new
life?[7] Since Plato's account of the Atlantis civilization in
Timaios and *Kritias* there have been numerous stories
about the sinking of an island and its utopian city.[8] Its
sinking is caused by natural disasters alone or by natural disasters brought on by the moral decline of the civilization.

Le Guin's story, although alluding to the Atlantis

myth in the title and in the concept of a city that has sunk into the sea, is not simply a retelling of one of the versions of the Atlantis story. Her narrative sustains itself in terms of characters, setting, and conflict. Le Guin, in fact, has distanced her story from Atlantis. She names Atlantis only in her title; thus she avoids asserting that either of the cities is the mythical Atlantis. She distances her story from the myth by setting the story on the Pacific coast. The tangential relationship between Le Guin's story and the legend of Atlantis is similar to the relationship between Le Guin's story and her contemporary world. Darko Suvin has argued that the story is a parable about Le Guin's "alienated world," a relationship of setting *one thing by the side of another,* the explicit by the side of the implicit."[9]

Le Guin juxtaposes the three worlds (the Atlantis legend, "the new Atlantis," the present consensus reality) to suggest that understanding one's self or society depends on recognizing its roots and its vision, its past and its future. But more importantly for her development of this fourth world, Le Guin the author is looking for its roots and the dreams. In *The Lathe of Heaven* Orr's frantic dreams simply allowed people to survive, and Haber's hyperrational vision turned the world into a gray, joyless place. In "The New Atlantis," even though she shows her West Coast being transformed by floods, earthquake, and volcanic eruptions, Le Guin is simultaneously discovering the voices of the past and the future, the voices of "the great souls, the great lives, the lonely ones, the voyagers" (76). The first-person point of view is used for both the Portland and the sea sections.

Significantly, the voices of the oppressors are not recorded. Their activities are, for the most part, occurring off stage, and when the government representatives do interact directly with Belle and Simon, Belle only summarizes what they say. Le Guin's decision to keep the voices of the oppressors out of the story also shows a maturity in her technique. In *The Lathe of Heaven* and the Hainish novel *The Word for World is Forest* Le Guin's oppressors are almost stereotypically evil; Davidson has no redeeming qualities and Haber has few. These two villains, especially Davidson, so emphasize the moral message that the message almost overwhelms the aesthetic and thematic interests.

In the context of Le Guin's West Coast world, "The New Atlantis" is a significant step in her search for the voices to describe a nontraditional utopia. Not only does she need a certain kind of character, but she also must find appropriate narrative techniques including narrative structure, point of view, and even the format of the printed page.

In *The Lathe of Heaven* Le Guin had used a narrative structure she developed in the previous Hainish novel, *The Word for World is Forest,* that of setting against each other people of opposing world views and philosophies. "The New Atlantis" more closely resembles the structure she used in the earlier novel *The Left Hand of*

THE WEST COAST

Darkness, in that she alternates between cultures that are remarkably different and yet share basic perceptions of reality and morality.

For this second dystopic view of the future American West Coast, Le Guin created a female protagonist and let her speak for herself. Belle's development is part of Le Guin's growing awareness of the distinctive female qualities. Certainly one can argue that most of Le Guin's protagonists, whether male or female (and the majority have been male), have displayed the characteristics of the female principle and that these characteristics are shown to be virtues in the resolution of the plots. These characteristics would include being accepting, nurturing, receptive, balanced, anarchic.

Although *The Tombs of Atuan* was a significant exploration of womanhood, Tenar was still an adolescent at the end of the novel. In *The Left Hand of Darkness* Le Guin explored the androgynous personality, trying to respond to her own heightened awareness of how gender characteristics are shaped by the sociopolitical environment. In *The Dispossessed* she tried to get past the abstract idea of the female principle and its manifestation in certain personality traits of men and women and to consider the distinctive characteristics of an actual woman in a particular environment. The fact that Takver remains a secondary character suggests that Le Guin was not yet comfortable with the female voice. But in *The Dispossessed*, Shevek praises women as natural anarchists.

This opinion is restated by Belle as she interacts with the black-market doctor she has found to treat Simon:

> She gathered very soon that Simon and I were married, and it was funny to see her look at us and smile like a cat. Some people love illegality for its own sake. Men, more often than women. It's men who make laws, and enforce them, and break them, and think the whole performance is wonderful. Most women would rather just ignore them. You could see that this woman, like a man, actually enjoyed breaking them (69).

Thus Le Guin reiterates her earlier belief about women in general but recognizes the differences among particular women. Belle is presented, not as the female principle, but as a unique woman. Le Guin sees in her the courage, vision, and artistry of a great voyager.

Central to Belle's survival is her refusal to be silenced. She keeps a notebook of how she copes with an upside-down world, and she expresses her vision of a better world in her music. By choosing the private journal, Belle aligns herself with women across many ages and lands who found the personal narrative (journal, diary, letter) their primary outlet for frustrated intelligence and talents. The poignancy of her sections, like that of women's diaries and letters, lies in her struggle to maintain integrity, self-respect, and creativity while surrounded by reminders of a government which

THE WEST COAST

enslaves its citizens by the services it provides, thus fulfilling the patriarchal model on which it is based.

Belle's music, rather than her notebook, has greater power to transform the world. The ocean people hear it and are renewed. In her own fragmented world, however, Belle's art is aligned with grief. It expresses the dream of a better world; but Simon and his friends with their working solar cell have no political power by which to revolutionize the availability of production and distribution of energy.

Belle's last section ends with news of her pregnancy and her plans of walking to Salem to see Simon; she fears they may treat him with drugs and behavior modification. Portland has been cut off from the rest of the West Coast by landslides and earthquakes; she will carry with her some dried food, "a tiny camp stove powered with the solar cell," her viola, and "a half pint of brandy." She concludes: "When the brandy is gone I expect I will stuff this notebook into the bottle and put the cap on tight and leave it on a hillside somewhere between here and Salem. I like to think of it being lifted up little by little by the water, and rocking, and going out to the dark sea" (86). Her last act is to preserve her voice and to imagine its continuance.

Alternating with Belle's notebook entries are the six sections, printed in italics and indented, told in the first-person collective voice of the people rising with their city from the sea. Geologically, the rise of new islands as a result of volcanic activity on the ocean floor or in trenches in the oceans, particularly the Pacific, is quite plausible, and the ocean people refer to rumbling sounds beneath them. Analogically, the geologic disturbances at the earth's roots are a response to the violation of the planet and its ecosystem by humankind. The awakening of the ocean people is a gradual process as the different senses are stimulated, beginning with sight; and Le Guin includes, in their descriptions, numerous allusions to death and rebirth, to past and present. As in the Gethenian creation myth which Le Guin wrote for *The Left Hand of Darkness,* their new life is accompanied by knowledge of mortality. When they describe what the emergence from the sea will be like, they use some of the same language that Simon's friend used to describe Belle's expressive music:

When we break through the bright circle into life, the water will break and stream white down the white sides of the towers, and run down the steep streets back into the sea. The water will glitter in dark hair, on the eyelids of dark eyes, and dry to a thin white film of salt (85).

In Belle's sections Le Guin found a voice to express both the demise of a West Coast civilization and the dream of a better world. In the ocean sections Le Guin is searching for and experimenting with a voice with which to create a utopia. Even in this very bleak forward look at her contemporary society Le Guin, like Belle, does not stop dreaming of a better way to go. The rediscovery by the ocean people of the physical details of their world is analogous to Le Guin's imaginative, careful discovery of a world in her imagination. But the difficulty she has in imagining a utopia on her own West Coast is reflected in the fact that the story ends before the city breaks through to the surface. Further, the closing lines of the story are spoken by the ocean people, and they lament the loss of the old world, Belle, and the other great dreamers: *"Where are you? We are here. Where have you gone?"* (86).

Suvin has argued eloquently that the ocean people represent the political alternative to "the ultimate class society of the corporate State" and its "pollution and ignorance of both self and universe." He asserts: "The Atlantis collective has been submerged and unconscious for ages, just as has the idea of a true and beautiful collective or classless society; the Fall of Atlantis, then, is here something like the fall from tribal into class society and the concomitant alienation of man into social institutions."[10]

In light of her next West Coast novel it is significant that in "The New Atlantis" Le Guin has turned to the past in her search for utopia, having rejected the modern Western version in *The Lathe of Heaven*. She turns to the voice from the past to see if it can speak with authenticity to her dream and to the present. The cuttlefish pointing to its own ancient carved image is an appropriate image of what Le Guin has accomplished in "The New Atlantis" in building the West Coast world of her fiction:

> *The moving thing clung or hovered there, above the door, like a swaying knot of silvery cords or a boneless hand, one arched finger pointing carelessly to something above the lintel of the door, something like itself, but motionless—a carving. A carving in jade light. A carving in stone.*
>
> *Delicately and easily the long curving tentacle followed the curves of the carved figure, the eight petal-limbs, the round eyes. Did it recognize its image?* (84).

Le Guin has caught both the old and new existing for a moment. And in that juxtaposition she has acknowledged that there is a vision which endures from past to present even through the cataclysmic changes of the rise and fall of nations.

Always Coming Home

Having found a female voice which could imagine and hope for an alternate world even as she dies in dystopia, Le Guin uses other female voices to create the open-ended utopia in *Always Coming Home*. A casual examination of the text reveals its experimental nature. It is a novel about the Valley people, a future society living in a geographically altered northern California.

THE WEST COAST

In her preface Le Guin informs her readers that "the main part of the book is their voices speaking for themselves," and a glance at the contents shows the variety of genres used by the voices—poems, songs, stories, histories, dramas, novel, romantic tales, sayings, and life stories. Interspersed among the Valley voices are analytical sections about the culture by a narrative voice who calls herself the editor, as well as journal-type entries where the editor calls herself Pandora. Slipcased with the first edition was a cassette tape, "Music and Poetry of the Kesh." Contradicting the reader's impression of fragmentation is Le Guin's declaration in the preface that this is a novel, that the "narrative" is the first 400 pages and that the "explanatory, descriptive pieces" can be found in the last 125 pages, "The Back of the Book."

That Le Guin had been thinking about voice, narrative form, and the nature of utopia is evident in two essays published in the early 1980s—one in *Critical Inquiry* (Autumn 1980) and one in *The Yale Review* (Winter 1983). The first essay was a speech at the Conference on Narrativity, University of Chicago, October 1979. Titled "It Was a Dark and Stormy Night; or, Why Are We Huddling about the Campfire?" it uses voices of past storytellers (chroniclers, Holocaust survivors, an anthropologist, a novelist) to explore the question posed in her title. Each voice guides her to a similar answer: that telling stories is part of the nature of being human; the stories bear witness to one's existence, help "pre-

UNDERSTANDING URSULA K. LE GUIN

vent our dissolution into the surroundings,"[11] and are a reason for courageously continuing to exist. When Le Guin points out that the Welsh poet whom she quotes uses a "radial" structure rather than the traditional beginning, middle, and end, the reader realizes that Le Guin has experimented with this same radial form for her essay, a structure which is "circling about, repeating and elaborating the central theme."[12] It is the structure she used in *Orsinian Tales* and will use in *Always Coming Home*.

"A Non-Euclidean View of California as a Cold Place to Be" was originally given as a speech in April 1982 in La Jolla, California; Le Guin was evidently already working on the new novel.[13] Le Guin draws on multiple voices to explore why society has lost its faith in utopia. She argues that the loss of faith in the "rationalist" utopia may be appropriate: "It seems that the imagination is trapped, like capitalism and industrialism and the human population, in a one-way future consisting only of growth." She continues: "Our final loss of faith in that radiant sandcastle may enable our eyes to adjust to a dimmer light and in it perceive another kind of utopia."[14] For Le Guin the route to that different kind of utopia is to "go backward," to look for another model; she asserts:

In order to speculate safely on an inhabitable future, perhaps we would do well to find a rock crevice and go backward. In order to find our roots, perhaps we should look for them where roots are usually found. At least the Spirit of Place is a more benign one than the exclusive and aggressive Spirit of Race, the mysticism of blood that has cost so much blood.[15]

In *Always Coming Home,* using primarily anthropology but also geology and computer science, Le Guin posits the following thought experiment: Let's say that after the death of the late-twentieth-century civilization, humankind and computers became independent of each other. The machines function as a vast network for the collection, storage, and collation of data. Human cultures develop, at least in northern California, most of which are self-sustaining and nonexploitive.

The Napa Valley of California is a place Le Guin regards as home, for her family owned a ranch there where she has spent nearly every summer. Her Valley people, the Kesh, have survived two twentieth-century disasters: first, a military-industrial civilization whose residues have poisoned the land and people's genes; and second, earthquakes which reshaped the western coastline, created an inland sea in California, and opened the Humboldt River in Nevada to the sea.[16] The Valley people live in concert with their environment; they are an agrarian, pacifist society, living in eight villages along the Na River, and each raised with intimate knowledge of every bluff, rock, tree, and mountain that constitute their homeworld. They have government by consent and a participatory religion. Other agrarian or nomadic peoples also live in the area, with whom the Kesh have trade agreements or acquaintance. In the past the people in the north, The Dayao (or Condors), were difficult neighbors for they wished to impose their authority throughout the Valley. The Dayao built cities and exploited the countryside for their technology of war for awhile. All groups have equal access, by terminals, to the City of the Mind, an extensive computer network (some 11,000 sites), left from the previous civilization.

Le Guin's desire "to speculate safely on the inhabitable future" calls to mind a similar expression she used to describe Shevek's desire for a better world in *The Dispossessed:* "the fragile, makeshift, improbable roads and cities of fidelity: a landscape inhabitable by human beings."[17] The contrast between the Hainish ambiguous utopia in *The Dispossessed* and the West Coast dystopias in *The Lathe of Heaven* and "The New Atlantis" suggests a dichotomy in Le Guin's own thinking about the nature of the literary utopia. This attraction to and criticism of utopia is also evident in the text of *Always Coming Home.*

The uniqueness of the novel in Le Guin's quest to "get to" utopia is that Le Guin was able to imagine an ambiguous utopia much closer to consensus reality than was Anarres. Her journey, as the creator of utopian texts, is one of always coming home. Further, the dialogue between utopist and critic is resolved only in this text. She boldly enters the text, argues with it, and is converted by it.

THE WEST COAST

The technique Le Guin chooses for letting the author coexist in the text with the characters and for drawing the reader into the making of the culture is to use the textual model of the ethnograph, in which both the voices of the anthropologist and the people being studied are heard. Ethnography is the first stage of an anthropologist's research. Claude Lévi-Strauss explains that it is the field work consisting of observation and description, "often with an exhaustive thoroughness" in an effort to record the "living reality" which the anthropologist has experienced.[18] Lévi-Strauss once described his "trunk full of documents relating to my fieldwork" as including "linguistic and technological card-indexes, a travel diary, anthropological notes, maps, diagrams, and photographic negatives—in short, thousands of items."[19] Ethnography also includes the tasks that immediately follow the field work: "the classification, description, and analysis of particular cultural phenomena—whether weapons, tools, beliefs, or institutions." The result is a text; Lévi-Strauss generalizes that the typical ethnograph "consists of a monograph dealing with a social group small enough for the author to be able to collect most of his material by personal observation."[20]

Always Coming Home is not an ethnograph, of course. It describes an imagined society; it lacks the objective tone of most anthropological writing, is not organized by traditional topics, includes mainly primary material and little analysis; and it allows the editor to enter the text in a number of self-reflexive passages. Because of its apparent fragmentation *Always Coming Home* is more like Lévi-Strauss's trunk than it is like the ethnograph that might have been published in *American Anthropologist*.

In this self-reflexiveness, however, Le Guin is acting like the anthropologist who writes a nontraditional ethnograph that is as much about the scientist's effort to write about the society as it is about the society being studied.[21] This "cross-dressing," one genre in the guise of another, in *Always Coming Home* obviously draws attention to the literary creative act and all that it entails— the writer, the audience, the social contexts of both, the subject and form of the story or poem, and sometimes the performance of the telling.

By calling attention to itself as an artifact, this novel blurs the distinction between fact and fiction, actual and imagined, process and product, artist and character, observer and participant. By writing a novel that is like an ethnograph Le Guin makes the fiction more factual and the fact more fictional. Using a known form of scientific writing makes her account of the Valley people more credible. The ethnograph is clearly scientific, and its subject is an actual, not an imagined, society. So the form makes the fiction more factual. The factual nature of the text, however, is also undercut by the form. The ethnograph, by its very nature, is a record of a temporary contact from which only temporary conclusions can be drawn. So the ethnograph form makes the "apparent" fact more fictional.

The ethnograph model not only makes more credible all the details (political, economic, scientific, aesthetic) about the Valley people, it also makes more credible the voices of the Valley people. The Valley people speak for themselves in the majority of the text and interact among themselves, especially in storytelling. For example, audience response influences the tale that is told; or an audience member becomes the next teller; or notes, additional material, corrective accounts are added to a written document preserved in one of the libraries. Furthermore, just as the anthropologist relies on key "informants," so the editor relies heavily on the people from one of the nine towns of the Valley, the town of Sinshan, particularly on a woman named Thorn.

Another level of interaction occurs in the reader's mind, as she or he tries to pick up common threads within or among sections. On this level of "intratextuality" the reader reenacts the experience of the anthropologist doing field work by listening to different informants, collecting stories and poems, checking maps, listening to the tape.

Le Guin models her novel on the scientific document, models her fictional characters on informants for anthropologists, and transforms the reader into an amateur anthropologist. *Always Coming Home* coherently calls attention to both society and art as artifacts. The self-reflexive nature of the novel is reinforced by the self-reflexive nature of sections where the editor frets over the novel she is trying to write or where the editor's characters discuss the nature of the novel with the editor. Le Guin's verbal self-reference is a little like M. C. Escher's visual self-reference in his drawing of the two hands which are drawing each other ("Drawing Hands"). Thus *Always Coming Home* is a novel about people telling stories and a novel about how the novelist is telling the story of people telling stories. It is a novel about people approaching a utopia, and it is a novel about how the novelist approaches utopia.

In his recent study *The Self-Conscious Novel: Artifice in Fiction from Joyce to Pynchon*, Brian Stonehill notes that one of the themes of the self-conscious novel is the power of the imagination "to transcend the stubborn facts of reality."[22] Le Guin's novel celebrates this power by emphasizing storytelling. The Kesh are expert, untiring storytellers. Stories may be jokes, teaching devices, ways to honor an animal, or ways to try to understand a memorable experience. The stories are frequently shared orally, a connection between speaker and listener referred to as "people breathing together."[23] The stories are sometimes written down and given to a lodge or to the Valley library in Wakwaha-na. The writer and reader are transformed:

THE WEST COAST

The trust or confidence that can be established between writer and reader is real, though entirely mental;
on both sides it consists in the willingness to animate,
to project one's own thinking and feeling into a harmony with a not-yet-existent reader or a not-present
and perhaps long-dead writer. It is a miraculous and
entirely symbolical transubstantiation (503).

Between storyteller and listener/reader is established a relationship analogous to that which makes
community possible. The give-and-take of the storytelling experience is in the model of "integration and
integrity," to use Le Guin's description of the goal of the
Hainish. Narrative art is to be valued not only for its
content, lesson, or entertainment but also for its ability
to replicate the communal experience. Because the nature of the Kesh utopia, if it is one, lies not in any
material prosperity but in its sense of community, storytelling is thus one way to approach utopia. Significantly, the only time the word *utopia* appears in *Always
Coming Home* is at the culmination of a conversation about
books which occurs between Pandora and the Archivist.

The narrative modes of the Valley are numerous,
and the only firm distinction the Kesh insist on is to
separate intentional lies from the rest. Narrative types
cannot be distinguished as fact and fiction. Rather, the
editor comments, "The kind of narrative that tells 'what
happened' is never clearly defined by genre, style, or

valuation from the kind that tells a story 'like what happened'" (500). The Kesh especially honor the life story, "a 'hinge' or intersection of private, individual, historical lived-time with communal, impersonal, cyclical being-time, . . . a joining of temporal and eternal, a sacred act" (263).

The longest story in the novel is a life story, divided into three parts and placed near the beginning, the middle, and the end of the narrative part of the book. It is the autobiography of the only Valley person to live with the Dayao. It covers not only Stone Telling's journey from childhood to maturity but also her physical journey to the city of the Condors where she lived for seven years and her return. Like Shevek in *The Dispossessed*, Stone Telling leaves her ambiguous utopia and lives among a people who define relationships in terms of dominance and submission. Even though she marries a Condor and bears him a daughter, she is never able to be at home with these warriors.

When she finally manages to escape and begin her walk home to the Valley, she calls herself Woman Coming Home; her goal is one all of her people share. The Kesh are, metaphorically, always coming home, always renewing their connection with the roots of their world. The goal of life is the process itself; their year is a series of celebrations, alternating between those of the sun and those of the moon. Living is analogous to being in the middle of the narrative; only when one is dead has the story ended.

THE WEST COAST

A shorter, but also notable, life story is that of Flicker of the Serpentine, who learns about the relationship between individual and the cosmos. Flicker's story is placed in the center of the novel. Since childhood she has experienced the nonrational world as a real presence, and she eventually enters training as a visionary. Her central vision, which she will spend the rest of her life recalling and interpreting and struggling to find words for, is the mystical experience of the one and the many, of unity and diversity. She attempts to explain it:

It was the universe of power. It was the network, field, and lines of the energies of all the beings, stars and galaxies of stars, worlds, animals, minds, nerves, dust, the lace and foam of vibration that is being itself, all interconnected, every part part of another part and the whole part of each part, so comprehensible to itself only as a whole, boundless and unclosed (290–91).

In these two women's life stories is illustrated the interplay of the three forms of energy which the Kesh spend their lives learning about: the cosmic, the social, and the personal.

In the life story Le Guin provides the Kesh voice speaking of individual, particular experience. Then, in the "Back of the Book," in the anthropologist's voice she provides the general, abstract discussion of the Kesh perception of the energies that make up the world. The reader approaches an understanding of this society or utopia by means of the particular story told by the specific storyteller, the one who had the experience.

Another voice that the reader engages with is that of the anthropologist/editor that Le Guin has chosen for the overall narrator of the novel. The creation of this voice is the act that enables Le Guin to be hopeful about the possibility of a better world here and now. What is significant is not that Le Guin is predicting this society but that through the telling she can imagine an alternative society and can pull the reader through the same experience. If humankind is, as Le Guin suggests in this novel, the stories that people tell, then the ability to imagine an alternative way to go is significant indeed.

Le Guin finds that one narrating voice is not enough; she uses six voices or roles: ethnologist, editor, translator, novelist, middle-aged housewife, and Pandora. They are voices that investigate the concrete "things" of this culture, for in the thing itself is to be found both the concrete and the abstract. As ethnologist she collects information through the scientist's methods of observation, interview, and hypothesis. She tracks down the meanings of unfamiliar words or concepts, observes ritual dances and interviews the participants, travels to the main library of the Valley, visits the old storytellers accompanied by her tape recorder. An example of a finished report can be found in the back of the book in the "Kinfolk" section, where she analyzes and charts kinship relationships. An example of the ethnologist at work gathering information can be found in

"Time and the City," where she becomes frustrated when she tries to get answers to her questions about how the Kesh view the City of Man, the civilization that preceded theirs and included the twentieth century.

Her questions are complicated by the fact that "people" in Kesh refers to animals, humans, rocks, and plants. Chronology is unimportant to the Valley people; linear time is an artificial way of keeping track of events. Their calendar follows the changes of the sun and moon in a series of seven celebratory festivals. She discovers that her own twentieth-century civilization is regarded as being "outside" the world. The Kesh try to explain to her about the outside world, primarily through stories about which the ethnologist comments, "I can't call them fruitless, although it was rather as if one went for grapes and returned with grapefruit" (153).

As editor she arranges the material that she has collected, supplies explanations and glosses, and selects representative stories—a chapter from a novel, several types of dramatic works, poems from the different rituals, four "romantic tales." She selects the maps to include or requests help from someone to have them redrawn, reoriented so a twentieth-century reader can understand them. As translator she translates from Kesh to English, and the text is dotted with her endnotes and headnotes. She provides a fifteen-page glossary at the end.

When Le Guin speaks of her role as novelist, she is most self-conscious. Sometimes she is didactic. The

UNDERSTANDING URSULA K. LE GUIN

Archivist of the Madrone Lodge at Wakwaha-na describes the book that results from this voice:

This is a mere dream dreamed in a bad time, an Up Yours to the people who ride snowmobiles, make nuclear weapons, and run prison camps by a middle-aged housewife, a critique of civilisation possible only to the civilised, an affirmation pretending to be rejection, a glass of milk for the soul ulcered by acid rain, a piece of pacifist jeanjacquerie, and a cannibal dance among the savages in the ungodly garden of the farthest West (316).

The other authorial voice appears more frequently; Le Guin names it Pandora and writes eight sections in her voice. These sections read like entries in a writer's notebook; she records her struggle to get "there," to fully understand the Valley perspective and way of life. Pandora's anxiety is understood not only in light of the destructive tendencies Le Guin sees in the contemporary world but also in light of her previous West Coast stories where she saw very little hope for humankind. Reading these nine sections as a unit, the reader sees the transformation that occurs in the narrator/anthropologist as she creates the Kesh world. Significantly, Thorn, her primary informant, is in training for midwifery and the care of "pregnant and nursing women" (474). Le Guin's text, then, nurtures both the Kesh and the new self of the author.

THE WEST COAST

The Pandora voice is at first angry, cynical, impatient, and frustrated. It is the voice of the critic of utopia, one who has rejected the Western, planned utopia and wants to believe in the open-ended utopia, but is so borne down by humankind's demonstrated ability for self-destruction that she is afraid to hope for a better world. It is the voice which dominated *The Lathe of Heaven* and "The New Atlantis." Her third section shows her anxiety: "Pandora Worrying About What She Is Doing: She Addresses the Reader with Agitation." Worried that her readers will criticize her for reducing the population of northern California and destroying civilization's knowledge, she acknowledges her historical and mythic heritage:

All I did was open the box Prometheus left with me. I knew what would come out of it! I know about the Greeks bearing gifts! I know about war and plague and famine and holocaust, indeed I do. Am I not a daughter of the people who enslaved and extirpated the peoples of three continents? Am I not a sister of Adolf Hitler and Anne Frank? Am I not a citizen of the State that fought the first nuclear war? Have I not eaten, drunk, and breathed poison all my life, like the maggot that lives and breeds in shit? (147–48).

Acknowledging that she cannot change history, she looks at the "hope" that lies at the bottom of Pandora's box and sees it as time. Time not only to read this novel, but also "time to look forward, surely; time to look back; and room, room enough to look around" (148), to consider alternative ways to go. In the Pandora voice can be heard Le Guin's previous female characters. All are subversive, natural anarchists. Further, they are all bringers of gifts. Pandora, especially as reinterpreted by the feminists, has become a bringer of knowledge.

Having faced her anxiety, Pandora is able, in the next section, to get fully inside the Valley, a world which she has alluded to earlier as "a big room, that holds animals, birds, fish, bugs, trees, rocks, clouds, wind, thunder. A living room" (148). Her near mystical experience occurs as she contemplates a scrub oak, a very particular piece of the Kesh living room. To be mindful in the Kesh society was to be aware of "the cosmic/social/self-relatedness of all existences," of the "interdependence of energies and beings, a sense of one's place and part in the whole" (490). To be part of the Kesh society, then, is to be immersed in the world. She consents to learn how to sing praise as the Kesh do, and the Back of the Book includes three poems that Pandora wrote in the Kesh style.

Toward the end of the novel Pandora says to the reader, "We have a long way yet to go, and I can't go without you" (339). She acknowledges, as the Kesh do, the importance of the audience in the creation of the story and the "transubstantiation" which occurs in the act of reading. She needs room and time to carry on a dialogue with the reader.

THE WEST COAST

The spirit or muse of all the storytelling in this novel is a female spirit honored by the Kesh, Coyote. In Kesh stories Coyote is involved with the coming of humans, the making of an environment suitable for them, and "allowing" them and their world to coexist with the other "people" and the wilderness. But Coyote stories reveal that not only is she a creator, she is also a destroyer; she is both wise and foolish, reverent and obscene. Such energy is like that of the storyteller who uses words to create people, places, events in the audience's mind, and to destroy the audience's conventional way of looking at things. Like Coyote the storyteller is disrespectful of conventions, and her energy may well appear to be irrational, perverse, unpredictable, meddlesome; in fact if the goal of the storyteller is to transform the reader, then the storyteller must act in this way.

The Coyote as trickster-god is a familiar figure in Native American tales, and Jung has argued that the trickster is a shadow figure whose function is to "undo the consolidation of consciousness" and keep "the door open for the influx of new creative contents."[24] In a more religious vein Joseph Epes Brown, a lifelong student of Native American lore, asserts that the trickster "opens a door, in a very subtle and effective way, into a realm of greater reality than the realm of the ebb and flow of everyday life."[25] Brown points out the two methods of opening doors in Coyote stories, shock and humor.

Coyote's shock and humor appear not only in the Kesh stories and in their treatment of the editor, but also in the editor's novel-ethnograph. The experience of reading *Always Coming Home* is an experience in "Coyote's house," for Le Guin defies expectations for plot and for a chronological narrative order. The self-reflexive sections and the radial ordering of the novel shock and amuse the reader. The separation of material into the narrative itself and the back of the book is, for some sections, an arbitrary decision. *Always Coming Home* makes fun of the convention that a novel is defined by its adherence to a recognizable form and narrative order. Joseph Epes Brown has commented that the trickster's levity during solemn ceremonies is "a shattering of the structure of the rite in order to get at the essence of the rite."[26]

Its fictionality revealed, the novel as artifact leads the reader to contemplate the essence of storytelling. People are "always telling stories," are always trying to understand and to relate and to connect the information, the facts and fictions of inner self and outer time and space. For the Kesh the visual image of connection is the double spiral with each arm ending or beginning (depending on one's perspective) in the same empty space. The artists, writes one of the Kesh poets, "go there with empty hands. . . . They come back with things in their hands" (74).

Always Coming Home is a novel with holes in it—

gaps between sections, stories, periods of time, between towns, between characters. By including mostly primary texts and a minimum of analysis, Le Guin thrusts the reader into the middle of the text, where the reader struggles to understand the other, both in terms of the Kesh way of life and in the nature of this novel. The experience between writer and reader is an exchange of gifts, analogous to the act which is the foundation of human community. And the exchange is transforming.

The writer, the people written about, and the people written to share an experience of human society; they all come to believe that human relationships are an experience not of product but of process, of always renewing and making new connections. *Always Coming Home* is very much like the most reflexive ethnographs where the anthropologist abandons the objective tone and the third-person point of view and describes how he or she gathered information and drew conclusions about the society being studied. Such accounts emphasize that what is valuable for both the storyteller and the anthropologist is not merely the final product (i.e., the statement of what is understood) but also the process (i.e., the unending changes, accommodations, making and unmaking that produce a novel or an ethnograph). In pursuit of knowledge of the other, each writer-character-reader-anthropologist pursues herself. Thus, in the journey from here to there, in the transformation (or transubstantiation) which occurs in Coyote's house, knowledge of the other and self is gained—all are always coming "home."

Coyote and Pandora say that if people can get from here to there in a story, then they have a chance to alter the "here" and "there" of consensus reality. Like the Kesh whose stories *are* their world, people have a chance to transform themselves and their society if they can tell a story about an alternate way of life.

Notes

1. Le Guin, A First Note, *Always Coming Home* (New York: Harper & Row, 1985).

2. Larry McCaffery and Sinda Gregory, "An Interview with Ursula Le Guin," *The Missouri Review* 7, no. 2 (1984): 76.

3. The following works, set outside the West Coast world, show Le Guin's continued concern with utopia: "The Ones Who Walk Away From Omelas" (1973), "Field of Vision" (1973), *The Dispossessed* (1974), "The Day Before the Revolution" (1974), "The Diary of the Rose" (1976). The first three short stories are in *The Wind's Twelve Quarters* (New York: Harper & Row, 1975); the last short story is in *The Compass Rose* (Harper & Row, 1982).

4. Le Guin, *The Lathe of Heaven* (New York: Avon, 1973) 82. Subsequent references will be noted in parentheses. I briefly discussed these mottoes in "The Middle-Landscape Myth in Science Fiction," *Science-Fiction Studies* 5 (1978): 136–38.

5. For an interpretation of the novel which stresses its relationship to Philip K. Dick, see Ian Watson, "Le Guin's *Lathe of Heaven* and

THE WEST COAST

the Role of Dick: The False Reality as Mediator," *Science-Fiction Studies* 2 (1975): 67–75.

6. Le Guin, "The New Atlantis," *The New Atlantis and Other Novellas of Science Fiction*, ed. Robert Silverberg (New York: Hawthorn, 1975) 85. Subsequent references will be noted in parentheses.

7. Charlotte Spivack, *Ursula K. Le Guin* (Boston: Twayne, 1984) 88.

8. See the comprehensive survey in L. Sprague de Camp, *Lost Continents: The Atlantis Theme in History, Science, and Literature* (New York: Dover, 1970).

9. Darko Suvin, "Parables of De-Alienation: Le Guin's Widdershins Dance," *Science-Fiction Studies* 2 (1975): 269.

10. Suvin 269.

11. Le Guin, "It Was a Dark and Stormy Night; Or, Why Are We Huddling about the Campfire?" *Dancing at the Edge of the World* (New York: Grove, 1989) 28.

12. "It Was a Dark and Stormy Night" 25.

13. "Ursula K. Le Guin—Down to Earth," *Locus* Sept. 1984: 56. Le Guin states she had been working on the novel for "two or three years."

14. Le Guin, "A Non-Euclidean View of California as a Cold Place to Be," *Dancing at the Edge of the World* 88.

15. "A Non-Euclidean View" 84.

16. Nora Gallagher, "Ursula Le Guin: In a World of Her Own," *Mother Jones* Jan. 1984: 23.

17. Le Guin, *The Dispossessed: An Ambiguous Utopia* (New York: Harper & Row, 1974) 295.

18. Claude Lévi-Strauss, *Structural Anthropology* (New York: Basic Books, 1963) 327.

19. Claude Lévi-Strauss, *Tristes Tropiques* (New York: Atheneum, 1974) 33.

20. Lévi-Strauss, *Structural Anthropology* 354–55.

21. For a discussion of these concepts see Jay Ruby, ed., *A Crack in the Mirror: Reflexive Perspectives in Anthropology* (Philadelphia: University of Pennsylvania Press, 1982).

22. Brian Stonehill, *The Self-Conscious Novel: Artifice in Fiction from Joyce to Pynchon* (Philadelphia: University of Pennsylvania Press, 1988) 31.

23. *Always Coming Home* 502. Subsequent references will be noted in parentheses.

24. Marie-Louis Von Franz, *Creation Myths* (Zurich: Spring, 1972) 63–64.

25. Joseph Epes Brown, "The Wisdom of the Contrary," *Parabola* 4, no. 1 (1979): 55.

26. Brown 56.

CHAPTER SIX

Recent Fiction: In the Middle of the Narrative

Since publishing *Always Coming Home* in 1985, Ursula K. Le Guin has been intensely creative, publishing a book of poems, two short story collections, five children's books, a novel, a nonfiction collection, and several short stories and essays.

In her fiction, she has used three of the four primary worlds—Earthsea, the Hainish world, and Orsinia—and has altered the fourth, the future American West Coast. In 1990, Le Guin published *Tehanu: The Last Book of Earthsea*; a Hainish story, "The Shobies' Story"; and an Orsinian story, "Unlocking the Air." In 1991 she published *Searoad: The Chronicles of Klatsand*, a collection of short stories set on a nineteenth- and twentieth-century American West Coast.

The recent fiction must be read not only in the context of the fictional world Le Guin created in the past but also in the context of the recent publications. The previous chapters have shown that in a new work Le Guin examines a familiar world from a new perspective;

as one of her characters stated in *The Dispossessed*, "You *can* go home again, . . . so long as you understand that home is a place where you have never been."[1]

Le Guin's 1989 nonfiction collection *Dancing At the Edge of the World* helps the reader of her recent fiction to follow her thinking and identify some of her sources. In these essays, speeches, and book reviews, Le Guin was critical of and angry with social and literary treatment of gender issues. She read feminist writers and critics who were "setting me free in my old age to learn my own language"[2] and who have "empowered me to criticize . . . my society and myself."[3] To describe her recent changes she used the metaphor of giving birth to herself.

I have argued elsewhere that *Dancing At the Edge of the World* offered a new perspective on Le Guin's four worlds, that in the fiction of Orsinia and the future American West Coast—two geographic areas directly connected to her own life—Le Guin advanced her ideas about narration, society, and gender, ideas that were often conceived in the other two worlds—Earthsea and Hainish planets. I concluded:

Reading her fiction world by world allows
us to follow a journey in which Le Guin has
periodically come home to give birth to a new
sense of herself as a writer and as woman. Orsinia,
her first world, was a place where she could
always go to see how people survived in the face
of "macho-mandarin" governments. Earthsea was

a safe haven for the woman who could not yet question the traditional, hierarchical, male world of fantasy literature. The Hainish universe allowed her the freedom to explore alternative political and biological structures as well as experiment with narrative form. The future American West Coast is the world where her re-visions of the nature of society and the nature of narration come together.[4]

This chapter will examine Le Guin's returns to and subversions of her four worlds—her continuing narrative journey from "here to there."

Tehanu: The Last Book of Earthsea

Tehanu overlaps *The Farthest Shore*, published eighteen years earlier, by about one year. In *Tehanu* Ogion dies; Arren is crowned King of Earthsea; a new Archmage is sought; and Ged, no longer a wizard, and Tenar, a widow with two grown children, are reunited after a twenty-five-year separation. Le Guin has commented that the fourth Earthsea novel completes the symmetry that had been left unbalanced; that the previous trilogy was "as perfectly shaped as a three-legged chair."[5] She had treated the adolescents Ged and Tenar and the adult Ged; the fourth novel treats the adult Tenar.

Besides these obvious connections, there are other ways in which Le Guin continues the Earthsea narrative in *Tehanu*. Le Guin again depicts the coming-of-age experience, and she uses the narrative rhythm of the earlier books.

She introduces a new child who approaches her coming-of-age experience as she begins to learn about gain and loss, about freedom, responsibility, and limitation in the relationships between self and other, self and world. As in *The Farthest Shore*, the coming-of-age experience also represents the cycles of change that occur throughout life. Ged and Tenar work through their particular middle-age challenges of change and growth; and the human species faces a possible re-combination of the qualities of people and dragons.

The pervasive cycle of change is reflected, as in the earlier Earthsea books, in the narrative rhythm. The first chapter is a prologue, introducing the agent of and the need for change; the next chapters develop the characters involved in the changes, alternating between their periods of activity and periods of contemplation and learning; and the last chapter carries the reader into an experience of the moment when an old cycle ends and a new one begins.

Despite these similarities, *Tehanu* "feels" different from the other Earthsea novels. One reviewer wrote that the novel "seems almost like a coda to the earlier Earthsea novels—a quiet reflection on the disparity between grand deeds and life's day-to-day challenges, seen from the perspective of maturity."[6] Another lamented, "Le Guin has chosen to punish her own readers for having loved other books she herself wrote."[7]

More to the point is another reviewer's comment: "Like the worker in Brecht's poem who asked, 'Who built the seven gates of Thebes?' Le Guin asks, by implication, who did the dishes for all those feasts in Tolkien?"[8] In *Tehanu* Le Guin subverts her previous depiction of Earthsea and the heroic fantasy tradition to which the earlier books belong. Le Guin's form of subversion is analogous to a painter's reversal of figure and ground. The artist chooses what is to be the figure or object of interest in the painting and what is to be its background. In *Tehanu* Le Guin brings the women out of the background of Earthsea and makes them the figures; she did not annihilate the old Earthsea and create a new one as the reviewer implied when he lamented the loss of the Earthsea he loved.

The differences result from Le Guin returning to Earthsea after eighteen years of writing, reading, publishing, and—more recently—after the apocalyptic experiences of writing her fourth world. The "perspective of maturity" is both that of the author Le Guin and of the focal character Tenar. *Tehanu* shows a different side of Earthsea: the setting is the island of Gont, more specifically the houses Tenar frequents, separated by no more than a two-day walk or a few hours' sea journey; the agents of change are women; the mages and their hierarchical society are backgrounded while the family unit is foregrounded; and the concept of artistry is expanded to include more than wizardry.

The setting for *Tehanu* is small. Not only are there no long sea journeys, there is no seat of proclaimed power on Gont comparable to the School for Wizards on Roke, the palace for the King on Havnor, the cities of dragons in the western islands, or the temple of the God-King on Atuan. But Tenar, being a skilled housekeeper and, therefore, choosing to care for the dying, the homeless, and those scarred by fear and pain, finds herself at the center of a web of conflicting and changing powers that will transform Earthsea as fundamentally as any of the acts by the protagonists responding to any of the seats of power in the previous three novels. The novel's focus on the domestic scene as the nexus of power and change is reinforced by the novel's narrative voice. The omniscient narrator in *Tehanu*, in contrast to the previous three novels, rarely goes beyond the viewpoint and knowledge of the villagers of Gont. The setting and voices of *Tehanu* are those of a woman's world.

By depicting women as the agents of change and the bearers of wisdom, and by detailing the dialogue among mature women, Le Guin brings to the foreground what she had suggested about the unique perspective of women in *The Tombs of Atuan*. Tenar, who rejected a role society demanded she play, has a unique perspective on society in contrast to Ged and Arren, who have been educated and tested so as to fit into the roles society needs them to fill. Further, women who

RECENT FICTION

experience the conflict between private and public identities also have a unique perspective on individual identity. In *Tehanu* Ged and Tenar have exchanged the roles of teacher and pupil they held in *The Tombs of Atuan.*

The difference between male and female knowledge and power is evident in the contrast of Tenar with Ged and the Masters of Roke, and is the subject of several conversations between Tenar and Moss, the village witch. This contrast is central to Le Guin's subversive view of Earthsea, for it exposes the unquestioned assumptions about male supremacy in Earthsea. Tenar realizes that Master Windkey simply cannot hear her when she suggests that the "woman on Gont" they are looking for may be a woman of power herself and not the mother or sister who will lead them to a man of power. She muses, "How could he, who had never listened to woman since his mother sang him his last cradle song, hear her?"[9]

Tenar finds a similar lack of experience with women in Ged, who seems unconcerned that he cannot remember who raised him. Moss's explanation for a man's difference is that he is "like a nut in its shell . . . full of grand man-meat, manself. And that's all. That's all there is. It's all him and nothing else, inside" (56).

The domestic setting and the emphasis on women as sources of wisdom and change contribute to another notable difference between *Tehanu* and the previous trilogy. Le Guin subverts the dominant structure for human relationships in Earthsea by placing the mages and their hierarchical, male society in the background and bringing forward the family unit as the "figure." This subversion highlights the extent to which *Tehanu* is about the nature of power.

In the novel's prologue, when Tenar accepts the responsibility of rearing Therru she acknowledges the influence of the Dark Powers but focuses on dealing with the human manifestation of that evil. Tenar vows to the burned and suffering child, "I served them and I left them. . . . I will not let them have you" (5). In a recent interview Le Guin asserted that "The child is this element that was not present in the earlier books of Earthsea, of absolute irreparable injustice about which nothing can be done, even by a wizard."[10]

In the novel, as Tenar grapples with various powers, she comes to realize that no form of power is guaranteed to be free from abuse. For example, in discussing with Ged the fear in male-female relationships, Tenar wishes for power based on trust: "If it [power] weren't all these arrangements—one above the other—kings and masters and mages and owners—It all seems so unnecessary. Real power, real freedom, would lie in trust, not force." And Ged replies, "As children trust their parents" (221), at which point they are both silent. For in their relationships with their parents Ged, Tenar, and Therru were not taught trust and none was free from abuse.

Indeed, the problematics of the origin and use of power are inescapable, as illustrated in Ogion's story of

RECENT FICTION

the woman of Kemay which Tenar tells to Therru and, later, to Ged. The woman of Kemay is the source of the information that, at the beginning of Earthsea, dragons and humans were one race. But because "in time nothing can be without becoming," the one being was differentiated into two, as some of the dragon-people "became more and more in love with flight and wildness" and others "gathered up treasure, wealth, things made, things learned" (12). Each group wished to dominate the other; Tenar reports, "Those that were strongest, wild or wise, were those who killed each other first" (13).

Juxtaposed to these discussions are Tenar's activities as housekeeper and homemaker. In the face of evil and suffering and injustice, she acts according to her own moral principles and chooses to make room for herself and others to live fully, which to her means "having your work to do, and being able to do it" (106). Tenar works out in daily, human relationships the lessons that she, Ged, and Arren learned in *A Wizard of Earthsea*, *The Tombs of Atuan*, and *The Farthest Shore*. The family unit in general is not a guarantee against the abuse of power, but the family unit in particular can be free of the abuse of power.

The wisdom Tenar has acquired is particularly credible in that homemaking was never something she could take for granted. She is wise in empathy and courtesy and adept in her art of fulfilling responsibility toward those who need care and teaching. Consequently

Tenar is the one who recognizes that a great change is coming in Earthsea, that to repair and heal and restore the old powers, as the Mages suggest, is no longer sufficient.[11]

Tenar's insight is characteristic of the last major difference between *Tehanu* and the earlier Earthsea novels. In *Tehanu* Le Guin provides a greater variety of figures of the artist than she did in the trilogy. Tenar herself suggests this broader vision when she prods Ged to recognize that wizardry is closed to women as an option and then asks, "Magic means the skills, the arts of wizards, of mages?" Ged responds, "What else would it mean?" and Tenar asks, "Is that all it could ever mean?"(95). In the portrayal of the artistry of women—Tenar, the village witch Moss, and Therru—Le Guin subverts two aesthetic assumptions that had been unchallenged in the previous Earthsea novels: the heroic fantasy tradition and the language of the androcentric society.

Like her literary foremothers, especially Virginia Woolf, Le Guin found that the traditional literary form could no longer house her characters or her concept of art. For the first three Earthsea novels, Le Guin wrote in the heroic fantasy tradition. Her stories depicted the initiations and quests of a male hero whose success gained him a prominent position in the male hierarchy of power. Women appeared only as background figures, useful as mothers, early teachers, or tempters manipulated by evil forces. The mature artist Tenar could not exist in such a world.

RECENT FICTION

Furthermore, although village witches were usually women in the trilogy, their limited powers were acknowledged in the saying, "weak as woman's magic, wicked as woman's magic." In *Tehanu* these women artists are allowed to speak for themselves. Tenar realizes that Moss's "obscurity and cant . . . was mere ineptness with words and ideas. . . . Nobody had ever listened to what she said" (54). By conversing with her, Tenar learns about the differences between a man's power and a woman's power. Moss states: "Ours is only a little power, seems like, next to theirs. . . . But it goes down deep. It's all roots. It's like an old blackberry thicket. And a wizard's power's like a fir tree, maybe, great and tall and grand, but it'll blow right down in a storm. Nothing kills a blackberry bramble" (110).

In the character of Ged, Le Guin also shows how difficult it is for an artist to shift out of the androcentric mode. Ged has been locked in the shape of wizard and Archmage for so long that when he begins life on Gont without his powers, he despairs and even wishes for death. As he works into his new sense of identity, he recognizes the shortcomings of the mages: "The men on Roke trust themselves and one another. Their power is pure, nothing taints its purity, and so they take that purity for wisdom. They cannot imagine doing wrong" (221).

The mages' inability to imagine a different perspective illustrates the second aesthetic assumption that

Le Guin has exposed about Earthsea. The people and their leaders are locked into an androcentric language. Therefore, the new artistry must involve the use of a different language. Therru, descendant of the dragon-people, will be the source of that different language. In name it is Old Speech; she is the only being in human form who speaks that language without having to learn it. Figuratively, the different language, like her very being, is a meld of elements that complement each other. She is related to those beings that the woman of Kemay described who left Earthsea "till they came to the other side of the world. There they live in peace, great winged beings both wild and wise, with human mind and dragon heart" (13).

In her "Bryn Mawr Commencement Address" of 1986, included in *Dancing*, Le Guin discussed the need for a new language. Drawing on her readings of feminist critics, she first defined "the father tongue" and "the mother tongue." The father tongue is "the language of power—of social power." Although this language of public events "is immensely noble and indispensably useful, [w]hen it claims a privileged relationship to reality, it becomes dangerous and potentially destructive."[12] In contrast, "the mother tongue" is the language used when women offer their experience as truth; it is used to describe ordinary events, work, and people and is used as conversation whose function is to connect and exchange. Finally, Le Guin writes, there is a third language, the language of art when you hear the coming together, the marriage of the public discourse and the private experience, making a power, a beautiful thing, the true discourse of reason. This is a wedding and welding back together of the alienated consciousness that I've been calling the father tongue and the undifferentiated engagement that I've been calling the mother tongue.[13]

The new artist, then, is one who is able to transform the old stories. In Ovid's *Metamorphosis,* transformation was most often a form of punishment for the person who saw too much; in *Tehanu* transformation is a reward for the person who sees much. Therru's true name identifies this basic nature of the artist: "Tehanu" means the Eye of the Swan, the bird that is an emblem of transformation.

"The Shobies' Story"

Le Guin's interest in language that exposes and blends "the public discourse and the private experience" is also evident in her latest Hainish story. In "The Shobies' Story" Le Guin weaves together concepts about storytelling from the old Hainish world and from her current interests. The story is part of her thinking about how stories are made. In a recent interview she asserted: "readers, after all, are making the world with you. You give them the materials, but it's the readers who build that world in their own minds. I am very aware of writing as a collaborative act."[14] The connection between "Shobies" and the previous Hainish works is so close that "The Shobies' Story" could begin with the opening two paragraphs of *The Left Hand of Darkness*, in which Genly Ai explains his assertion, "I'll make my report as if I told a story, for I was taught as a child on my homeworld that Truth is a matter of the imagination."[15] Le Guin has stated that she feels "back home out there, playing around" with the "far future, Hainish universe."[16]

Set in the Hainish world some time after the people of Gethen have joined the Ekumen, "The Shobies' Story" focuses on a space exploration crew made up of Gethenians, Terrans, Hainish, and a Cetian from Anarres. The ten crew members have chosen to be the first humans to experience instantaneous space travel, or "transilience."

Despite the focus on space exploration, this story—published sixteen years after Le Guin's last Hainish story—is not about the Hainish reconnecting with one of their seeded planets. There is no "alien" culture; there is no heroic, solitary emissary or scientist taking risks to establish contact. Further, the metaphoric quality of the crew's experience is more dominant than in previous Hainish stories. Metaphorically, the story is about the experience of telling (or writing) and hearing (or reading) stories; transilience is also the leap from consensus reality to the fictive world.

As space adventure the story involves the crew's preparation for, experience of, and report on transilience. The story is similar to the previous Hainish works in technique and style. Le Guin focuses on a technological invention that affects communication among worlds, she continues to explore nonhierarchical sociopolitical structures, and she uses the space voyage as an analogue for the journey into the self.

Le Guin plays with the overemphasis on complex technology that occurs in some science fiction, satirizing the technical jargon and the belief that equipment alone will solve human problems. Discussions of the churten drive, a console with "an on-off switch,"[17] and transilience are also discussions of the relationship between technology and other aspects of human culture. At one point, Gveter the Anarresti suggests that "to churten, we—we conscious ones—maybe it depends on our consciously perceiving ourselves as . . . as transilient—as being in the other place—the destination?" (60). In other words, not only does the culture's belief in the need for a tool help bring the tool into existence, the effectiveness of the tool is determined by the nature of the culture's belief in it. The tool must be integrated into the human culture.

The first test of the crew, who call themselves "Shobies" after the name of their ship *Shoby*, is whether or not they can achieve "the psychic interbalance of a bonded social group" (43). In the nearly five weeks the crew has together before the journey, they are

successful. Their "affective focus" or hearth is the pair
of Gethenians and their two children; the crew's ritual
of building a campfire and gathering around it to discuss transilience or to tell stories is both a cause and an
effect of their bonding.

As a space crew, they operate by consensual decision and their model is "a network of response," rather
than "a chain of command" (47). But after transilience
the Shobies experience being in "no-time"; their instru-
ments are not functioning and they cannot agree on
what they perceive. For example when the NAFAL nav-
igator Lidi tries to tell concretely what she perceives,
she says "I can see the stars through the walls" (51); un-
nerved and embarrassed by what she thinks is her failure she isolates herself from the group. Their network,
by nature, is so fragile that they lose their "thread,"
their "crewness."

In their first efforts to reestablish their network
and assimilate the experience of transilience, the Shobies persuade Lidi to return and all try to tell concretely
what happened. Failing, they then try the ritual of
storytelling. The story that each Shoby tells is personal;
it reveals what the transilience meant to that person.
But it is simultaneously a public story, in the sense that
each story reveals the person's relationship to the crew
and to some aspect of the larger Hainish society.

In order for the Shobies to tell their story, they
must reestablish themselves with relation to time. Thus,
when Sweet Today orchestrates the telling she asks

one of the children, "how does a story begin?" The answer, "A thousand winters ago, a thousand miles away," initiates the sense of time for the Shobies (61–62). They continue creating that sense of time by telling the story in the past tense. They also create a sense of themselves being in time by distinguishing between the self which is telling the story and the self that experienced no-time and lost the thread. Each speaker uses the third person pronoun. For example, Lidi tells her story as follows: "Although she wished . . . she realized that she really hoped the thing wouldn't work, because it would make her skills, her whole life, obsolete . . . all the same she really wanted to learn how to use it, too, if she could, if she wasn't too old to learn . . ." (62).

In her story, Lidi articulates her fear of growing old, of not being able to do her "work"—what she personally enjoys and what makes her a contributing member of her society. Her difficulty in expressing what she knows is shared by the other Shobies for whom the space journey has also been a journey into the self. Telling their story enables the Shobies to remain sane, assimilate their experience, and survive; their multivoiced story will become their official report on transilience.

Metaphorically, the space adventure is the fiction adventure; transilience is the experience of entering the fictive world by way of the imagination—the sensations of consensus reality, including an awareness of

UNDERSTANDING URSULA K. LE GUIN

"real" time, are suspended. "The Shobies' Story" depicts the pleasures and difficulties of telling and interpreting stories.

Le Guin's sense of play in doubling is evident. For example, the story alludes to several of her other writings as when one of the characters refers to "Shevekian temporalism" (*The Dispossessed*) and another notes that members of the early space crews were often crazy ("Vaster Than Empires And More Slow"). The ritual of the campfire echoes Le Guin's well-known essay "It Was a Dark and Stormy Night; or, Why Are We Huddling about the Campfire?" There are also amusing time doubles. The Shobies are in "nonexistence" for forty-four minutes, which is about the time it would take to read the story; and the Shobies' trip has been to a planet seventeen light-years away, which is approximately the number of actual years between the composition of the last Hainish story and this one.

Le Guin also plays with language, devising descriptions of the churten drive in pseudotechnical language which actually makes sense when applied to the adventure of fiction. In the name for the technology which makes transilience possible—the churten mode—Le Guin plays with verbal ambiguity, calling attention to the complexities involved when people try to verbalize their experiences. The churten mode or drive is a metaphor for the mental faculty, including the imagination, that enables humans to "enter" a world that is not physically present. "Churten" suggests "certain"; but what kind of certainty might be an attribute of the imagination? Textual allusions to Pascal, Plato's allegory of the cave, and the anthropologist's method of thick description further complicate the concept of certainty and enhance the irony of the phrase "the churten drive."[18]

This speculation about the relations among reality, experience, and expression are reflected in the characters' reactions to the adventure of fiction. Frustrated and confused, the individuals abandon the attempt to reach agreement on what "really" happened. They shift from the report mode to the story mode, whereupon the arguments diminish. To tell their stories, they try to connect their experiences with "the here and now." In the interaction between teller and listener, the personal story becomes the public story. The public nature of the story is enhanced by the way the telling is presented to the reader of "The Shobies' Story." The telling is a performance; voices, not named individuals, speak. And the reader who has been "listening" closely to these voices throughout the story can identify nearly every voice.

The success of the story mode demonstrates the centrality of narration in human culture. In her essay "Some Thoughts on Narrative" Le Guin made the following distinction between report and story:

In recent centuries we speakers of this lovely language have reduced the English verb almost entirely to the indicative mood. But beneath that specious and arrogant assumption of certainty all the ancient, cloudy, moody powers and options of the subjunctive remain in force. The indicative points its bony finger at primary experiences, at the Things; but it is the subjunctive that joins them, with the bonds of analogy, possibility, probability, contingency, contiguity, memory, desire, fear, and hope: the narrative connection.[19]

The conclusion of "The Shobies' Story" reiterates the significance of storytelling. When the Shobies greet the "anxious scientists, engineers, and officials of Ve Port and the Ekumen," the Shobies are asked, "What happened?" The story concludes, "And the Shobies looked at one another and said, 'Well, it's quite a story. . . .' " (64). Their report will be in story form where multiple voices remain distinct and yet an integration of meaning is achieved. Indeed, the narrative voice of "The Shobies' Story," speaking in the past tense with the third person pronoun as if telling of an event long ago in time and space, is the voice of the Shobies themselves—the story we read is the Shobies' report on transilience.

"Unlocking The Air"

Published in 1990, fourteen years after *Orsinian Tales* (twelve years after *Malafrena*), "Unlocking The Air"

RECENT FICTION

is recognizably Orsinian. The country is still politically oppressed and, by implication, affected by the Communist Party that dominates Central Europe; the Orsinians desire autonomy and self-determination, symbolized by free elections. The characters are members of the Fabbre family who were featured in "Brothers and Sisters" (dated 1910) and "A Week In The Country" (dated 1962). Set in November 1989, "Unlocking The Air" depicts Bruna and Stefan Fabbre, now twenty-seven years older than they were in "A Week In The Country," married and parents of a daughter who is a student leader in the Orsinian independence movement.

"Unlocking The Air" is also recognizably a recent Le Guin story. Like "The Shobies' Story," it focuses on the significance of storytelling; like *Always Coming Home* it is a self-reflexive text. The narrative voice, more prominent than in the preceding Orsinian stories, tells the story of the Fabbres and tells about telling this story.

In the last decade, in a variety of public forums, Le Guin has called for readers and scholars to consider issues that arise when the universality of storytelling is considered. In 1979 at the University of Chicago's symposium "Narrative: The Illusion of Sequence," Le Guin gave the closing presentation. In the context of previous presentations by narratologists such as the deconstructionist Jacques Derrida, the psychoanalyst Roy Schafer, the historian Hayden White, and the art critic Nelson Goodman, Le Guin announced her thesis as follows:

The *histoire* is the what
and the *discours* is the how
but what I want to know, Brigham,
is *le pourquoi*.
Why are we sitting here around the campfire?[20]

In a lecture at Portland State University in 1980 she continued her exploration of the function of stories and asserted that "Narrative is a central function of language.
Not, in origin, an artifact of culture, an art, but a fundamental operation of the normal mind functioning in
society. To learn to speak is to learn to tell a story."[21]

Applying her belief in narrative as a mode of freedom and moral choice, in her 1989 SFRA Pilgrim Award
Acceptance Speech she called on scholars and teachers
to avoid arguments about the generation of prescriptive
definitions of literary genres. Rejecting the canon and
the concept of "high" and "low" genres, she urged:

What's important to me is not setting up these polari-
ties and rivalries, but getting free of them. I want us
to be unquestionably free to work without penalty in
any mode or genre of fiction we want, and to cross
from one to another, and to crossbreed them, too. I
believe that a lively literature is nourished not by purity but by promiscuity.[22]

In "Unlocking The Air," using different writing
styles, Le Guin calls attention to the artificiality of fairy

RECENT FICTION

tale, history, and story. She uses a number of the techniques which have become associated with what Brian Stonehill has called the "self-conscious" story.[23] The narrator speaks to the reader in her or his role as reader, refers to the process of selecting information to include in the story, and calls attention to the text the narrator is creating. Le Guin calls attention to the structuring of the text by dividing it into fourteen sections, all but one of which she begins with the narrator's declaration of a subject; for example, each of the first four sections begins, respectively, "This is a fairy tale." "This is history." "This is a stone." "This is a story."[24] The theme of both levels of her story (the Fabbre story and the narrator's story) is the relation between reality and fiction.

The title of the story comes from the weekly, peaceful protest by the Orsinians in Krasnoy who gather in Roukh Square across from the Palace and shake their keys in the air. In a 1990 interview, when asked for her response to the events in Eastern Europe, Le Guin responded, "What I feel is fiction. I'm a story writer and my response to that is a short story which is a sort of combination of rejoicing and mourning. Joy and fear."[25] The context for the Fabbre story of November 1989 is the challenge to the Communist Party's domination of Central and Eastern Europe and Asia. The events of 1989 were particularly dramatic: the Tiananmen Square protest in Beijing in May and June; the end of the Communist majority in the government in Hungary in

October; and the opening of the border between East and West Germany in November.

The older Fabbres, permanently scarred by the deaths of their family members in previous periods of resistance—Bruna's brother Kasimir, Stefan's grandfather and father—are afraid to hope or work for change. However, their daughter Stefana, "a graduate student in the department of Orsinian and Slavic Literature, working for a degree in the field of early romantic poetry" (102), is a member of the Committee of the Student Action Council which is planning the revolution.

At the heart of the Fabbre story is a section that highlights the issue of the relation between fiction and reality. It details a committee meeting in which Stefana and the members argue about how far into the future they need to plan. Their use of the imagination to develop political alternatives and consider their consequences (i.e., to use fiction to alter reality) contrasts sharply with Stefan Fabbre's assertion that he wants to ignore the circumstances outside his biology lab and simply do his research. In effect, if Stefan continued to ignore the revolution, he would be replacing reality with fiction. That Stefan is on the verge of making the wrong moral choice is underscored by the contrast between his and his daughter's work and attitudes. Stefana's research and her political involvement are related; the actions discussed at the committee meeting sound like a practical application of ideas in a poem by Percy Bysshe Shelley, one of the poets who might have influenced or resembled the Orsinian romantics that Stefana is studying. But Stefan risks an ironic rift between his research and his political choice. On the one hand, he seems prepared to withdraw from the generation of new life via the revolution going on outside his lab; on the other hand, he is engaged in research on RNA, ribonucleic acid, a polymer involved in protein synthesis. Found universally in living cells, RNA is one of the keys to life and may have been the original genetic material.

In the story of the narrator's process of writing, the narrator is similarly concerned with the relation between reality and fiction, particularly as shown by the types of narration that the narrator uses in trying to tell the story—history, fairy tale, and story. These three types describe a spectrum of narration: the events which are sequenced in time are real (or actual) in history, imaginary (or possible) in story, and fantastic (or impossible) in fairy tale. By labeling the sections, the narrator breaks the reader's illusion (for example, the illusion of objectivity in history or the suspension of disbelief in fiction) and calls attention to the artificiality that all narrations share—the imposition of or adherence to a form. Simultaneously, by creating believable characters and realistic dilemmas, the narrator invites the reader to suspend disbelief and enter into the pleasure of experiencing the fictional world. The narrator in "Unlocking The Air" teaches the reader to identify both the artificiality and the pleasure of the text.

UNDERSTANDING URSULA K. LE GUIN

The narrator reveals some of the similarities among history, fairy tale, and story. They all create an account by using "things" in consensus reality (and so some of the sections begin with the narrator naming a thing: stone, bus) and by using conventional narrative signals and figurative language. For example, the conventional opening and ending tags of fairy tales also appear in the sections labeled history ("once upon a time" and "they lived happily ever after"). The section that begins "This is a stone" could be part of any of the three types of narrative; the final section could be the conclusion of history, fairy tale, or story: "This is the truth. They stood on the stones in the lightly falling snow and listened to the silvery, trembling sound of thousands of keys being shaken, unlocking the air, once upon a time" (204).

Besides teaching the common attributes of narratives, the narrator, by using three different forms of narration, teaches the reader to consider the differences among the forms. Three limitations of history and fairy tale stand out—they portray people only as generalities, they do not portray women fully, and they cannot portray the future. True to the story's sense of play, the narrator exaggerates the characteristics of history and fairy tale in order to bring out these limitations.

People in the history and fairy tale sections are identified by their roles in a traditional androcentric, hierarchical society—king, soldiers, the people. In the history sections, no women appear. In the fairy tale sections, the narrator mentions a "maiden" and implies that she is merely a bargaining chip in the whole process of breaking the evil enchantment. Contrastingly, in the Fabbre story, the narrator creates unique, "flesh and blood" individuals and depicts a female leader of the revolution in Stefana Fabbre. When Stefana takes Bruna down to the Square for the weekly, peaceful protest by "the people," the narrator depicts the event from Bruna's perspective.

In contrast to story, neither history nor fairy tale can present a narration about the future. History can only record what has already happened. The narrator starkly presents this characteristic in the history sections by using a series of short sentences, each containing one piece of information, and by not linking the sentences together by any relationship other than the temporal one. Similarly, fairy tale, by convention, can never go beyond "and they lived happily ever after." The narrator calls the bargain by which the evil enchantment is broken a "betrayal": "Remember the moment when the betrayal is made, and ask no questions." The king "ruled long and well," but "Do not ask what the maiden received as her reward" (204).

In story, however, the narrator and the characters themselves can imagine what actions they might perform and what the consequences will be. The narrator comments, "But we can tell the story over, we can tell the story till we get it right" (204). This flexibility of story is demonstrated in both stories that the narrator tells. In the Fabbre story, at the committee meeting, the young people debate whether or not to bring in Rege, a former government leader, to form the new government and whether or not to accept aid from the West. Similarly, the narrator has imagined the narrative of the Fabbres being told as history, then as fairy tale, and finally as story. She even modifies story by introducing the crucial section that contains the committee debates as "This is a love story." Thus the narrator suggests that even the forms of story must be revised to contain all that she wants to say. In a world where "the real thing" for many people has become two seconds of images on the television screen, "the love story" becomes the best form in which to portray the fidelity that motivates Stefana Fabbre to participate in the revolution.

The final section of the story ends with the conventional tag beginning of fairy tales: "once upon a time." By this gesture, the narrator reiterates the need for continuing to retell the story, that each story is the beginning of a new story, that in making each new story, aspects of old stories may be incorporated and changed. In "Some Thoughts On Narrative," Le Guin explained "the narrative connection" as follows: "As J. T. Fraser puts it, moral choice, which is to say human freedom, is made possible 'by language, which permits us to give accounts of possible and impossible worlds in the past, in the future, or in a faraway land.' "[26]

Just as surely as the physical keys are transformed into symbols of resistance and freedom, so the fictional account of a better life can be transformed into an imaginary and then a physical reality. The necessary but elusive relation between word and thing, mind and body, is also that between fiction and reality.

Searoad: Chronicles of Klatsand

Klatsand, the setting for the short stories in *Searoad*, is not one of Le Guin's "faraway" lands and yet, because the stories focus on people not usually thought of as heroic, Le Guin is once again subversive as she establishes the narrative connection. Between 1987 and 1991 Le Guin published mainstream short stories with a shared setting—the northern Oregon coastal town of Klatsand. Adding a prologue and a novella, she published the collection in 1991. These stories are not science fiction or fantasy; however, they are an important element of the context of her recent publications, and including them in this chapter affords an opportunity to comment on at least one example of the relation between Le Guin's other publications and her fantasy and science fiction.

Although the collection is not fantasy, it is like *Tehanu* in its focus on the family unit. Although not science fiction, it is like the Hainish works in drawing its narrative idea and structure from contemporary science. Although not creating a complete country and its centuries-long political struggle, it is like the Orsinian stories in focusing on the common people. Like the future American West Coast stories and all of the latest works, including *Dancing at the Edge of the World*, the Klatsand stories articulate the woman's perspective.

There is no textual connection between *Searoad* and the science fiction stories of the future American West Coast beyond the shared coastal setting and the few indications in the background of the Klatsand stories that Americans are capable of severely diminishing the quality of their own lives. Furthermore, unlike Le Guin's other fourth world stories, the *Searoad* stories are not set in a future time, they are not based on end-of-the-world scenarios, and they are not part of Le Guin's ongoing discussion of utopia/dystopia.

However, the *Searoad* stories are related to the concerns and narrative techniques of the fourth world books. As I argued in "The Land-Lady's Homebirth: Revisiting Ursula K. Le Guin's Worlds," in her home-world settings Le Guin "breaks through cultural assumptions about gender, society, and literature."[27] These new stories are similarly subversive. In exploring the experience of older women, they revise an ancient female myth, expose the limitations of androcentrism, and experiment with point of view and structure.

The Klatsand stories, in content and technique, develop older characters who are—in fairly quiet, private ways—involved in a quest quite different from that of Le Guin's younger protagonists. In her book *Archetypal Patterns In Women's Fiction*, Annis Pratt discusses the differences between the two kinds of quests. She first quotes Carol Christ's distinction between the "social quest" of the *Bildungsroman* and the "spiritual quest" of the older character. The first is a "search for self in which the protagonist begins in alienation and seeks integration into a human community where he or she can develop more fully"; the second is the "self's journey in relation to cosmic power or powers. Often interior, it may also have communal dimensions."[28] Pratt notes how the two quests are experienced by women:

If the purpose of the novel of development is to integrate the individual into her society, its generic function is frequently aborted by society's unwillingness to assimilate her. The older woman hero, in contrast, has "been through all that"; her goal is to integrate her self with herself and not with a society she has found inimical to her desires.[29]

The setting of the *Searoad* stories reflects Le Guin's focus on older women and signals to the reader to be aware of androcentric society's dismissal of their value. On the one hand, the town seems to be an appropriate setting for people who have been judged "unimportant" by the people of power and influence. Klatsand is a small coastal town with limited economic opportunities for its primarily white residents. It is probably modeled on towns such as Cannon Beach (where Le Guin has a second home) and the northern Oregon area where Native Americans such as the Clatskanie tribe once lived. Klatsand's population is fairly stable. Tourists occasionally spend a night in one of its three motels; regular summer visitors rent or own old beach houses; and a new resident infrequently moves in seeking anonymity or a haven from the pressures of, for example, an abusive marriage or city life.

On the other hand, the people of Klatsand live in daily contact with one of the planet's most pervasive forces—the Pacific Ocean. They live, as one of the early white settlers put it, at "the end of the world."[30] Such a dramatic vision of one's environment is appropriate for the older characters that Le Guin creates in *Searoad:* the ocean traditionally symbolizes the passage of time, dynamism and transition, birth and death, generation and destruction. This double view of the setting operates on other aspects of the *Searoad* stories. On the one hand, the people in these stories are very ordinary people encountering common experiences; on the other hand, these are very important people because they encounter universal human experiences and, as women, are usually responsible for assisting others through them—experiences such as procreation and death, oppression and failure, abuse and sacrifice, injustice and compassion, and broken promises and unrealized dreams.

This discussion will focus on "Hernes," a novella that concludes *Searoad,* reflects many of its themes, demonstrates its experimental techniques, and articulates a re-vision of the myth of Persephone which then functions as the book's mythic correlative of the older woman's quest. "Hernes" is about the differences and interactions among four generations of women in one family—Fanny Crane Shawe Ozer (1863–1919), Jane Shawe Herne (1887–1968), Lily Frances Herne (1912–1966), and Virginia Herne (1929–).

In their first-person sections, these women tell their own experiences as their truths. The women cannot be easily described; consequently, the novella challenges both patriarchy's restricted assessment of women and feminism's monolithic view of women.[31] For example, Fanny Crane Shawe Ozer exhibits both socially defined "female" and "male" characteristics. She never questions that a woman should become a wife and mother; but the people she is responsible for die (her sister, both husbands, her son) or fail in her eyes (her daughter's marriage ends in divorce). Her son's death in 1918 in World War I teaches her the hollowness of men's aggrandizement of war, that becoming a soldier turns a boy into a man. But she also realizes that having money and owning property like the men in town do will give her security; so she eventually buys half-interest in the store, as well as two other pieces of property in Klatsand. She becomes the town's postmistress and is successful in getting the town named Klatsand. But her act of naming the town does not, for her, demonstrate her power; it acknowledges the area's first people. When Fanny first moved to the area in 1898 she met one of the few survivors of the five Native American villages that once flourished in the area; and the woman, who claimed her name was also "Fanny," told her that Klatsand was the name of the place.

The diversity of the *Searoad* women, the families they shape, and the values they hold often emerge in cross-generational relations. These are exemplified in "Hernes" in the life of Virginia Herne and her relation with her mother Lily and her grandmother Jane.

For example, Virginia Herne rejects her marriage to David when he tries to control what she does best—write poetry. She describes the patriarchy of which marriage is one institution as "the country of the other":

I wandered in his kingdom, a tourist, sightseeing—a stranger, bewildered and amazed—a pilgrim, hopeful, worshipful, but never finding the way to the shrine, even when I read the signposts that said Love, Marriage, and followed the highroads beaten wide by a million feet. A failed crusader, I never got to the holy place. . . . Ashamed, I left that country, his great, old country, stowed away, sailed off to the new world. And there I sought the new life. (174–75)

Virginia acknowledges her grandmother and her mother as "her mothers": "A strong woman whose strength is her solitude, a weak woman pierced by visionary raptures" (159). Neither of her mothers would have said what Virginia did about marriage, would have identified society as patriarchal, or would have spoken out for woman's freedom even though neither had a fulfilling marriage. Her grandmother Jane Shawe Herne left her husband, Lafayette Herne, when he failed to remain faithful, left San Francisco, and returned to Klatsand to rear her young daughter Lily. But she did not divorce Lafayette until he requested the action several years later, and she criticized independent choices made by both Lily and Virginia, acknowledging "I guess we think when a woman's free she's wrong" (173).

Lily Herne's weakness comes partly from internalizing patriarchy's view of women. Her adolescent daydream of her marriage consisted of the details of the wedding and the newspaper account but nothing about her life as a married woman. Her acceptance of society's view that a woman's goal is to marry affords her no resistance to the advances of Dicky Hambleton, who impregnates her when she is sixteen. She seems to fear life's activity and complexity and remains in Klatsand with her mother to rear her daughter Virginia. Her interactions with the angels of her visions, however, testify to Lily's independence, strong spirit, and imagination.

Virginia, Lily, and Jane—these constitute a family. And the family in "Hernes" and in other *Searoad* stories is the place where differences are negotiated, where the gap between self and other is acknowledged as sacred space, where domination can be refused.

UNDERSTANDING URSULA K. LE GUIN

At the heart of the novella as well as the whole collection is Virginia Herne's re-vision of the myth of Persephone. Traditional stories about Persephone include several elements attractive to a feminist like Virginia: a strong mother-daughter relation; a quest by the mother for the daughter; a reunion that transforms or rejuvenates the world; a recognition of original female power usurped by the male gods; and representation of life's stages in a Triple Goddess personified as maiden, mother, and crone. In her revisions Virginia continues Demeter's and Persephone's lineage, stating that Persephone had a daughter, conceived in the rape by the King of Hell. Virginia describes the transformative power of the mother-daughter relation as they make a family and share "all the housekeeping of the world" (155). But Virginia also describes the patriarchal society's continuance of the King of Hell's violent actions against women. Persephone, seeing the modern acts of violence against women, hastens back to Hell, saying to the King, "I divorce you, King of Dung." By refusing to be dominated, Persephone challenges the very foundation of patriarchy. Hell becomes chaos and she wins back her existence in the world of light, becoming "the woman of foam" in the sea (190).

Virginia's ability to find her voice, to write the story of Persephone which has some parallels to her own life, is rejuvenating. She wrote the first revision in the same year she published what she believed was an unsatisfactory second books of poems (1957); she wrote the

second revision in 1975 shortly before she began publishing four successful books of poems, culminating
with *Persephone Turning* (1983) which won the Pulitzer
Prize for poetry.

In this re-vision Le Guin gives the novella and the
book itself a mythic correlative of the quest of the older
woman. The women in stories such as "In and Out,"
"Hand, Cup, Shell," and "Quoits" all struggle to recognize what is important to them and find voices to reject what is not their truth. These women protagonists
of *Searoad* follow the advice Le Guin herself was once
given: "offer your experience as your truth."[32]

Besides challenging ideas about gender and society, Le Guin also challenges ideas about narrative in
"Hernes." The story is told in thirty-one sections that
alternate among five voices—an omniscient narrator
and the four Herne women. The dated sections range
from 1898 to 1979 but are not arranged in chronological
order. Further, at the end of the story, the chronology of
each woman's life is listed in a section titled "Biogra-
phies." The reader experiences a story of multiple perspectives and radial structure.

Drawing on techniques she used in *Orsinian Tales*
(the juxtaposition of time periods and the radial structure) and *Always Coming Home* (the lifestory and multiple points of view), Le Guin creates a narrative that
shows the network of connections among four succes-
sive lifestories and moves beyond the single-voiced,
first-person narrative.

The basic narrative movement of "Hernes" is not the resolving of a conflict but the weaving of a tapestry revealing life as perceived and experienced by four generations of the women of one family. Le Guin's desire to hold the details about these four women in a single narrative reflects ideas she expressed in her 1986 essay, "The Carrier Bag Theory of Fiction," ideas which are an example of the convergence of artists' and scientists' interest in the field concept.

In the essay (as in "Hernes") Le Guin makes clear that she sees this type of narrative as a reflection of women's experience of life. Her title comes from her appreciation of Elizabeth Fisher's theory that human civilization evolved from the first cultural artifact being not a weapon but a receptacle—a sling or a net in which to carry an infant or gathered food.[33] The novel or story which functions like a carrier bag is not about conflict or the male killer seen as hero, Le Guin asserts. It includes conflict, but its main subject is the "continuing process" of "things in a particular, powerful relationship to one another and to us."[34] Furthermore, such a story can best be told by abandoning the "linear, progressive, Time's-(killing)-arrow mode by Techno-Heroic."[35]

The structure of "Hernes" is indeed that of a carrier bag. For example, in the opening four sections the reader hears the voice of Fanny one year after she has moved to the coast (1898; age 35), then of Fanny's great-granddaughter Virginia thirteen years after Virginia has returned to Klatsand (1979; age 50), then of Fanny again, dying of flu (1919; age 56), and then the voice of Lily, Virginia's mother and Fanny's granddaughter, as a child growing up in Klatsand (1918; age 6). The themes of loss and creativity, of childhood and old age, of the spirit of place, and of the significance of woman's interpretation of life are all interwoven in these opening four sections.

Le Guin's use of the image of the carrier bag to explain her concept of woman's story is akin to the use of the image of the web to explain contemporary interest in the field concept. In *The Cosmic Web* N. Katherine Hayles uses the web as a metaphor for ideas about reality shared by artists and scientists. The web suggests that reality is "dynamic, holistic," including "objects, events, and observer," while simultaneously suggesting that the web of words cannot capture that which is always changing and is not differentiated into subject and object.[36]

In *Searoad*, then, as in *The Dispossessed* and *Always Coming Home*, Le Guin's narrative structure converges with ideas in contemporary science that enable her to acknowledge—as she had one of her characters state in an early Hainish story—that although no permanent harmony can ever be achieved, "the pleasure is in trying."[37] The carrier bag that is "Hernes" juxtaposes past, present, and future in an attempt to tell the lifestory of four generations of women and avoid a reductive causal interpretation of their interconnection.

UNDERSTANDING URSULA K. LE GUIN

In a related aspect of her narrative technique in "Hernes," Le Guin finds the single-voiced, first-person narrative to be inadequate for telling an intergenerational lifestory of women. Le Guin, along with a number of other contemporary women writers, seems to be reassessing how best to represent women's relation to a stratified social order. Adalaide Morris in "First Person Plural in Contemporary Feminist Fictions" has recently distinguished the stance of contemporary women writers from their predecessors. In the 1960s and 70s, she asserts, women wrote stories with a "room of one's own" plot to counter the "heterosexual romance plot." The stories focused on a woman searching for a unified feminine self and often used the first person point of view where the speaking "I" was the "existential I" whose goal was to define her place in the existing institutions and linear narratives. Recent authors have found the "existential I" to be "bounded," limited and isolated in its own room and therefore ineffectual for affecting society. Authors are experimenting with strategies whereby the room is replaced with the home and the existential I with the "I/i" (a personal and nonunitary self).[38] This view of the self, Morris asserts, is a "self-in-coalition," a self involved in "multiple connections that make us all divided and contradictory beings";[39] and she notes the relation between this approach and field theory. Contemporary writers use a narrative voice that speaks in first person plural as an attempt to establish, within the story and within the reading of the story, a coalition among reader, writer, and characters.

In "Hernes" Le Guin achieves a coalition of belief among reader, writer, and characters by having multiple and equal points of view. Le Guin's goal is similar to that of the authors Morris analyzes: not to resolve multiple perspectives into a single truth but to "respect their irreducible plurality."[40]

In the 1990s Le Guin has returned to three of her four primary worlds and has returned to the fourth but in a different century. Coming to them after writing many intervening pieces, including the apocalyptic novels of the fourth world, Le Guin, like the new Persephone, finds ways to re-envision her fictional worlds, the journey of the older woman character, and the nature of fiction. Her most recent work can be described with the words Le Guin has used to describe one of the central acts of language in fiction—"a continual weaving and restructuring of the remembered and the perceived and the imagined."[41]

Notes

1. Le Guin, *The Dispossessed: An Ambiguous Utopia* (New York: Harper & Row, 1974) 48.

2. Le Guin, "Bryn Mawr Commencement Address," *Dancing at the Edge of the World: Thoughts on Words, Women, Places* (New York: Grove, 1989) 151.

UNDERSTANDING URSULA K. LE GUIN

3. Le Guin, "The Fisherwoman's Daughter," *Dancing at the Edge of the World* 234.

4. Elizabeth Cummins, "The Land-Lady's Homebirth: Revisiting Ursula K. Le Guin's Worlds," *Science-Fiction Studies* 17 (1990): 163–64.

5. David Streitfeld, "Book Report: Le Guin's Worlds," *Washington Post Book World* 20 May 1990: 15.

6. Jim Creighton, "The Grand Sweep of Epic Fantasy," *St. Louis Post-Dispatch* 6 May 1990: D 5:3.

7. John Clute, "Deconstructing Paradise," *Times Literary Supplement* 28 December 1990: 1409.

8. Meredith Tax, "Fantasy Island," *Village Voice* 30 October 1990: 75.

9. Le Guin, *Tehanu: The Last Book of Earthsea* (New York: Atheneum, 1990) 160. Subsequent references will be noted in parentheses.

10. Beatrix Campbell, "Dark Star" [Interview], *Marxism Today* Nov. 1990: 4.

11. Le Guin discussed the unique wisdom of the mature woman in "The Space Crone," first published in 1976. See *Dancing at the Edge of the World* 3–6.

12. Le Guin, "Bryn Mawr Commencement Address" 147, 149.

13. Le Guin, "Bryn Mawr Commencement Address" 152.

14. Nicholas O'Connell, "Ursula K. Le Guin," *At The Field's End: Interviews With Twenty Pacific Northwest Writers,* ed. Nicholas O'Connell (Seattle: Madrona, 1987) 33.

15. Le Guin, *The Left Hand of Darkness* (New York: Harper & Row, 1980) 1.

16. Darrell Schweitzer, "Interview With Ursula K. Le Guin" [Part 1], *Science Fiction Review* 1 (Summer 1990): 24.

17. Le Guin, "The Shobies' Story," *Universe 1,* ed. Robert Silverberg and Karen Haber (New York: Doubleday, 1990) 43. Subsequent references will be noted in parentheses.

18. One of the characters quotes Pascal: "The heart has its reasons, which reason does not know" (39). The crew's inability to test their perception of what "really" happened calls to mind Plato's al-

RECENT FICTION

legory, particularly in the following: "Tai gestured at the cave of fire-light around them and the dark beyond it. 'Where are we? Are we here? Where is here?' " (61). "Thick description" (47) produces an ethnograph which describes a cultural event so as to reveal the mean-ing of the specific event or ritual and the meaning of the culture in which it is embedded.

19. Le Guin, "Some Thoughts on Narrative," *Dancing at the Edge of the World* 44.

20. Le Guin, "It Was a Dark and Stormy Night: or Why Are We Huddling about the Campfire?" *Dancing at the Edge of the World* 23.

21. Le Guin, "Some Thoughts on Narrative" 39.

22. Le Guin, "Spike the Canon," *SFRA Newsletter* no. 169 (July/August 1989): 17–21.

23. Brian Stonehill, *The Self-Conscious Novel: Artifice in Fiction From Joyce to Pynchon* (Philadelphia: University of Pennsylvania Press, 1988).

24. Le Guin, "Unlocking The Air," *Playboy* 37 (December 1990): 100. Subsequent references will be noted in parentheses.

25. Campbell, "Dark Star" 4.

26. Le Guin, "Some Thoughts on Narrative" 44.

27. Cummins, "The Land-Lady's Homebirth" 155.

28. Annis Pratt, *Archetypal Patterns in Women's Fiction* (Blooming-ton: Indiana University Press, 1981) 135–36.

29. Pratt, *Archetypal Patterns* 136.

30. Le Guin, *Searoad: Chronicles of Klatsand* (New York: Harper Collins, 1991) 129. Subsequent references will be noted in parentheses.

31. For an overview of some feminists' reductive view of women, see Jeanne Costello, "Taking The 'Woman' Out of Women's Autobiography: The Perils and Potentials of Theorizing Female Sub-jectivities," *Diacritics* 21 (Summer-Fall 1991): 123–34.

32. Le Guin, "Bryn Mawr Commencement Address" 150.

33. Le Guin, "The Carrier Bag Theory of Fiction," *Dancing at the Edge of the World* 166.

34. Le Guin, "The Carrier Bag Theory of Fiction" 169.

35. Le Guin, "The Carrier Bag Theory of Fiction" 170.

36. N. Katherine Hayles, *The Cosmic Web: Scientific Field Models and Literary Strategies in The Twentieth Century* (Ithaca: Cornell UP, 1984) 15–28.

37. Le Guin, "Winter's King," *The Wind's Twelve Quarters* (New York: Harper & Row, 1975) 106.

38. Adalaide Morris, "First Persons Plural in Contemporary Feminist Fiction," *Tulsa Studies in Women's Literature* 11 (Spring 1992): 11–29.

39. Morris, "First Person Plural" 15.

40. Morris, "First Person Plural" 23.

41. Le Guin, "Some Thoughts on Narrative" 44.

BIBLIOGRAPHY

Works by Ursula K. Le Guin
Novels and Novellas

Rocannon's World. New York: Ace, 1966; London: Universal-Tandem, 1972.

Planet of Exile. New York: Ace, 1966; London: Universal-Tandem, 1972.

City of Illusions. New York: Ace, 1967; London: Gollancz, 1971.

A Wizard of Earthsea. Berkeley: Parnassus, 1968; Harmondsworth: Puffin, 1971.

The Left Hand of Darkness. New York: Ace, 1969; London: Macdonald, 1969.

The Tombs of Atuan. New York: Atheneum, 1971; London: Gollancz, 1972.

The Lathe of Heaven. New York: Scribner's, 1971; London: Gollancz, 1972.

"The Word for World is Forest." *Again Dangerous Visions I*. Ed. Harlan Ellison. Garden City, NY: Doubleday, 1972. Published as *The Word for World is Forest*. New York: Berkley, 1976; London: Gollancz, 1977.

The Farthest Shore. New York: Atheneum, 1972; London: Gollancz, 1973.

The Dispossessed: An Ambiguous Utopia. New York: Harper & Row, 1974; London: Gollancz, 1974.

"The New Atlantis." *The New Atlantis and Other Novellas of Science Fiction*. Ed. Robert Silverberg. New York: Hawthorn, 1975.

Very Far Away from Anywhere Else. New York: Atheneum, 1976. Published as *A Very Long Way From Anywhere Else*. London: Gollancz, 1976.

"The Eye of the Heron." *Millennial Women*. Ed. Virginia Kidd. New York: Delacorte, 1978; London: Panther-Granada, 1980.

Malafrena. New York: Putnam's, 1979; London: Gollancz, 1980.

243

BIBLIOGRAPHY

The Beginning Place. New York: Harper & Row, 1980. Published as *Threshold*. London: Gollancz, 1980.

Always Coming Home. New York: Harper & Row, 1985; London: Gollancz, 1986.

Tehanu: The Last Book of Earthsea. New York: Atheneum, 1990; London: Gollancz, 1990.

Short Story Collections

The Wind's Twelve Quarters. New York: Harper & Row, 1975; London: Gollancz, 1976.

Orsinian Tales. New York: Harper & Row, 1976; London: Gollancz, 1977.

The Compass Rose. New York: Harper & Row, 1982; London: Gollancz, 1983.

Buffalo Gals and Other Animal Presences. Santa Barbara: Capra, 1987; London: Gollancz, 1990.

Searoad: Chronicles of Klatsand. New York: Harper Collins, 1991.

Photo Book

Way of the Water's Going: Images of the Northern California Coastal Range. Text from *Always Coming Home*; photographs by Ernest Waugh and Alan Nicholson. New York: Harper & Row, 1989.

Poetry

Wild Angels. Santa Barbara: Capra, 1975.

Hard Words. New York: Harper & Row, 1981.

Wild Oats and Fire Weed. New York: Harper & Row, 1988.

Drama

King Dog. Santa Barbara: Capra, 1985.

Literary Criticism

The Language of the Night: Essays on Fantasy and Science Fiction by Ursula K. Le Guin. Ed. Susan Wood. New York: Putnam's, 1979. Rev. ed. London: Women's Press, 1989; New York: Harper Collins, 1992.

BIBLIOGRAPHY

Dancing at the Edge of the World. New York: Grove, 1989; London: Gollancz, 1989.

Edited Volumes

Nebula Award Stories II. New York: Harper & Row, 1977; London: Gollancz, 1976.

Interfaces, with Virginia Kidd. New York: Ace, 1980.

Edges: Thirteen Tales from the Borderlands of the Imagination, with Virginia Kidd. New York: Pocket Books, 1980.

For Children

Leese Webster. New York: Atheneum, 1979; London: Gollancz, 1981.

The Adventure of Cobbler's Rune. New Castle, VA: Cheap Street, 1982.

Solomon Leviathan's Nine-Hundred and Thirty-First Trip Around the World. New Castle, VA: Cheap Street, 1983.

A Visit from Dr. Katz. New York: Atheneum, 1988; London: Collins, 1988.

Catwings. New York: Orchard Books, 1988.

Catwings Return. New York: Orchard Books, 1988.

Fire and Stone. New York: Atheneum, 1989.

A Ride on the Red Mare's Back. New York: Orchard Books, 1992.

Fish Soup. New York: Atheneum, 1992.

Selected Uncollected Essays

"Prophets and Mirrors: Science Fiction as a Way of Seeing." *Living Light* 7 (Fall 1970): 111–21.

"The Crab Nebula, the Paramecium, and Tolstoy." *Riverside Quarterly* 5 (1972): 89–96.

"On Theme." *Those Who Can: A Science Fiction Reader*. Ed. Robin Scott Wilson. New York: New American Library, 1973. 203–09.

"Ketterer on *The Left Hand of Darkness*." *Science-Fiction Studies* 2 (1975): 137–39.

BIBLIOGRAPHY

"A Response to the Le Guin Issue." *Science-Fiction Studies* 3 (1976): 43–46.

"A Very Warm Mountain." *Parabola 5,* no. 4 (1980): 46–51.

"On Writing Science Fiction." *Writer 94* (Feb. 1981): 11–14.

"Introduction." *The Book of Fantasy.* Ed. Jorge Luis Borges. New York: Viking Penguin, 1988. 9–12.

"Foreword: By Her Loneself." *A Home-Concealed Woman: The Diaries of Magnolia Wynn Le Guin, 1901–1913.* Ed. Charles A. Le Guin. Athens, GA: University of Georgia Press, 1990. ix–xiv.

"Children, Women, Men, and Dragons." *Monad* 1 (Sept. 1990): 3–27.

"Spike the Canon." *SFRA Newsletter* no. 169 (1989): 17–21.

"Recreating Reality: Making It Happen for Your Reader." *The Writer* 104 (1991): 11–13.

"The Writer On, And At, Her Work [poem]." *The Writer On Her Work: New Essays in New Territory.* Ed. Janet Sternburg. Vol. 2. New York: Norton, 1991. 210–22.

Selected Interviews

Gallagher, Nora. "Ursula Le Guin: In a World of Her Own." *Mother Jones* Jan. 1984: 23–27, 51–53.

Gilbert, Dorothy. "Interview: Ursula K. Le Guin." *California Quarterly* Spring/Summer 1978: 38–55.

McCaffery, Larry, and Sinda Gregory. "An Interview with Ursula Le Guin." *The Missouri Review* 7, no. 2 (1984): 64–85.

O'Connell, Nicholas, ed. "Ursula K. Le Guin." *At the Field's End: Interviews with Twenty Pacific Northwest Writers.* Seattle: Madrona, 1987. 19–38.

Remington, Thomas J., and Robert Galbreath. "Lagniappe: Ursula K. Le Guin. An Informal Dialogue with Conference Participants." *Selected Proceedings of the 1978 Science Fiction*

BIBLIOGRAPHY

Research Association National Conference. Cedar Falls: University of Northern Iowa, 1979. 269–81.

Schweitzer, Darrel. "Interview: Ursula K. Le Guin." *Science Fiction Review* 1, no. 2 (1990): 22–24 and 1, no. 3 (1990): 52–56.

Searles, Baird. "Ursula K. Le Guin: The Lathe of Science Fiction." *Amazing* Sept. 1986: 41–46.

Walker, Paul. "Ursula K. Le Guin." *Speaking of Science Fiction: The Paul Walker Interviews.* Oradell, NJ: Luna, 1978. 24–36.

Ward, Jonathan. "Ursula K. Le Guin Interview." *Dreams Must Explain Themselves.* Comp. by Andrew Porter. New York: Algol Press, 1975. 30–37.

Books and Special Journal Issues

Bittner, James W. *Approaches to the Fiction of Ursula K. Le Guin.* Ann Arbor, MI: UMI Research Press, 1984. Close reading of her pre-1979 works which emphasizes complementarity as the literary form (the romance) and theme.

Bloom, Harold, ed. *Ursula K. Le Guin.* Modern Critical Views. New York: Chelsea House, 1986. Collection of previously published essays; of limited value because all documentation has been removed.

Bucknall, Barbara J. *Ursula K. Le Guin.* New York: Ungar, 1981. Admirer's summary and analysis of the fiction.

De Bolt, Joe, ed. *Ursula K. Le Guin: Voyager to Inner Lands and to Outer Space.* Port Washington, NY: Kennikat, 1979. First book collection of eight original essays on her critical reception and her science fiction and fantasy; includes biographical essay.

Olander, Joseph D., and Martin Harry Greenberg, eds. *Ursula K. Le Guin.* New York: Taplinger, 1979. Nine original essays on major patterns in her science fiction and fantasy.

BIBLIOGRAPHY

Selinger, Bernard. *Le Guin and Identity in Contemporary Fiction.* Ann Arbor: University of Michigan Press, 1988. Study of five novels in terms of psychoanalytic theory and the complexities of identity.

Slusser, George Edgar. *The Farthest Shores of Ursula K. Le Guin.* Popular Writers of Today: The Milford Series. San Bernardino, CA: Borgo, 1976. Monograph tracing increased complexity in theme and structure of her science fiction and fantasy.

Spivack, Charlotte. *Ursula K. Le Guin.* United States Authors Series. Boston: Twayne, 1984. Perceptive introduction to novels, short stories, criticism, and poetry.

Suvin, Darko, ed. "The Science Fiction of Ursula K. Le Guin." *Science-Fiction Studies* 2 (1975). Essays, primarily Marxist, on her science fiction; includes first significant bibliography.

Yoke, Carl B., ed. Special Ursula K. Le Guin issue. *Extrapolation 21* (Fall 1980). Ten original articles, evenly divided between major emphases in science fiction and in fantasy.

Uncollected Critical Articles about Le Guin

Abrash, Merritt. "Le Guin's 'The Field of Vision': A Minority View on Ultimate Truth." *Extrapolation* 26 (1985): 5–15. Reads the story as a subtle comment on *2001.*

Baggesen, Soren. "Utopian and Dystopian Pessimism: Le Guin's *The Word for World is Forest* and Tiptree's 'We Who Stole the Dream.' " *Science-Fiction Studies* 14 (1987): 34–43. Shows the stories both exemplify and clarify Ernst Bloch's distinction between two kinds of pessimism.

Barbour, Douglas. "Wholeness and Balance in the Hainish Novels of Ursula K. Le Guin." *Science-Fiction Studies* 1 (1974): 164–73. Discusses Taoist imagery in five Hainish works.

BIBLIOGRAPHY

Bickman, Martin. "Le Guin's *The Left Hand of Darkness:* Form and Content." *Science-Fiction Studies* 4 (1977): 42–47. Persuasive analysis of unity of form and content.

Clemens, Anna Valdine, "Art, Myth and Ritual in Le Guin's *The Left Hand of Darkness." Canadian Review of American Studies* 17 (1986): 423–36. Delineates significance of ritual and matriarchal myths in the novel.

Collins, Jerre. "Leaving Omelas: Questions of Faith and Understanding." *Studies in Short Fiction* 27 (1990): 525–35. Examines why a political reading of the story is not efficacious.

Cummins, Elizabeth. "The Land-Lady's Homebirth: Revisiting Ursula K. Le Guin's Worlds." *Science-Fiction Studies* 17 (1990): 153–66. Discusses her recent nonfiction in the context of her four fictional worlds.

Delany, Samuel R. "To Read *The Dispossessed." The Jewel-Hinged Jaw.* Elizabethtown, NY: Dragon Press, 1977. 239–308. Criticizes discrepancies between novel's ideas and its scenes.

Erlich, Richard D. "Ursula K. Le Guin and Arthur C. Clarke on Immanance, Transcendence, and Massacres." *Extrapolation* 28 (1987) 105–29. Contrasts the authors' views on humanity's aggression and authoritarianism.

Getz, John. "A Peace-Studies Approach to *The Left Hand of Darkness. Mosaic* 21 (1988): 203–14. Discusses the novel as an example of peace-studies principles.

Hull, Keith N. "What Is Human? Ursula Le Guin and Science Fiction's Great Theme." *Modern Fiction Studies* 32 (1986): 65–74. Illustrates that defining what is human is a dominant science fiction theme in Le Guin's fiction.

Jose, Jim. "Reflections on the Politics of Le Guin's Narrative Shifts." *Science-Fiction Studies* 18 (1991): 180–97. Focuses on differences in narrative technique and alternative societies between *The Dispossessed* and *Always Coming Home.*

BIBLIOGRAPHY

Klein, Gerard. "Le Guin's 'Aberrant' Opus: Escaping the Trap of Discontent." Trans. by Richard Astle. *Science-Fiction Studies* 4 (1977): 287–95. Analyzes Le Guin's avoidance of discontent and pessimism through cultural relativism and plurality.

Le Clair, Tom. "Ursula Le Guin's *Always Coming Home.*" *The Art of Excess: Mastery in Contemporary American Fiction.* Urbana: University of Illinois Press, 1989. 204–37. Novel is one of seven masterworks which excel in world view, narrative techniques, and effect on readers.

Parrinder, Patrick. "The Alien Encounter: Or, Ms. Brown and Mrs. Le Guin." *Science-Fiction Studies* 6 (1979): 46–57. Examines the issue of characterization in science fiction.

Philmus, Robert. "Ursula Le Guin and Time's Dispossession." *Science Fiction Roots and Branches.* Ed. R. J. Ellis and Rhys Garnett. New York: 1990. 125–50. Demonstrates how Shevek's achievement of a general temporal theory validates theme and form of *The Dispossessed* and of the Ekumen.

Roemer, Kenneth. "The Talking Porcupine Liberates Utopia: Le Guin's 'Omelas' as Pretext to the Dance." *Utopian Studies* 2, nos. 1 & 2 (1991). Argues that the ones who walk away from Omelas are not privileged; followed by responses from several scholars.

Shippey, T. A. "The Magic Art and the Evolution of Words: Ursula Le Guin's Earthsea Trilogy." *Mosaic* 10 (1977): 147–63. Perceptive analysis of language issues in the Earthsea trilogy.

Spencer, Kathleen. "Exiles and Envoys: The SF of Ursula K. Le Guin." *Foundation.* no. 20 (1980): 32–43. Uses anthropologist Victor Turner's concept of liminality in analyzing three of Le Guin's works.

BIBLIOGRAPHY

Stone-Blackburn, Susan. "Adult Telepathy: *Babel-17* and *The Left Hand of Darkness.*" *Extrapolation* 30 (1989): 243–53. Uses two novels to argue that telepathy is a metaphor for psychic growth.

Tavormina, M. Teresa. "Physics as Metaphors: The General Temporal Theory in *The Dispossessed.*" *Mosaic* 13 (1980): 51–62. Clarifies relationship between the novel and Shevek's theories of time.

Walker, Jeanne Murray. "Rites of Passage Today: The Cultural Significance of *A Wizard of Earthsea.*" *Mosaic* 13 (1980): 179–91. Argues that reading the novel becomes a rite of passage for the modern adolescent.

Wood, Susan. "Discovering Worlds: The Fiction of Ursula K. Le Guin." *Voices For The Future: Essays on Major SF Writers.* Ed. Thomas D. Clareson. Bowling Green, OH: Bowling Green University Popular Press, 1979. 2: 154–79, 204–05. Uses fantasy and science fiction to prove that web imagery describes both the protagonist and the artist.

Bibliography

Cogell, Elizabeth Cummins. *Ursula K. Le Guin: A Primary and Secondary Bibliography.* Boston: G. K. Hall, 1983.

Currey, L. W. "Bibliographic Checklist of the Works of Ursula K. Le Guin." *The Language of the Night.* New York: Harper Collins, 1992. 240–49.

INDEX

The index does not include references to material in the notes.

INDEX

INDEX

INDEX

INDEX

INDEX

INDEX

INDEX

INDEX

INDEX